"COLOR-BLIND"
RACISM

This book is dedicated to all those who gave
of their lives and all those who gave
their lives in this struggle.
They are not forgotten.

"COLOR-BLIND" RACISM

Leslie G. Carr

SAGE Publications
International Educational and Professional Publisher
Thousand Oaks London New Delhi

For information:

SAGE Publications, Inc.
2455 Teller Road
Thousand Oaks, California 91320
E-mail: order@sagepub.com

SAGE Publications Ltd.
6 Bonhill Street
London EC2A 4PU
United Kingdom

SAGE Publications India Pvt. Ltd.
M-32 Market
Greater Kailash I
New Delhi 110 048 India

Printed in the United States of America

Library of Congress Cataloging-in-Publication Data

Carr, Leslie G.
    "Color-blind" racism / by Leslie G. Carr
        p. cm.
    Includes bibliographical references (p.) and index.
    ISBN 0-7619-0443-3 (cloth: acid-free paper).—ISBN
0-7619-0444-1 (pbk.: acid-free paper)
        1. United States—Race relations. 2. Racism—United States.
    3. Race discrimination—United States. 4. Afro-Americans—Race
    identity. 5. Afro-Americans—Civil rights. I. Title.
    E185.615.C3515 1997   97-4840
    305.8'00973—dc21

This book is printed on acid-free paper.

            99 00 01 02 03 10 9 8 7 6 5 4 3 2

Acquiring Editor:	Peter Labella
Editorial Assistant:	Corinne Pierce
Production Editor:	Astrid Virding
Production Assistant:	Karen Wiley
Typesetter/Designer:	Danielle Dillahunt
Indexer:	L. Pilar Wyman
Cover Designer:	Candice Harman
Print Buyer:	Anna Chin

CONTENTS

INTRODUCTION

About 15 years ago, a group of conservative intellectuals began developing the argument that because the constitution is "color-blind," liberal policies, such as affirmative action, were unconstitutional. They argued that it was not legal for the government to take race into account in a "color-conscious" manner. This argument has become the basis for a series of Supreme Court decisions that have undermined affirmative action and, more recently, called into question the legality of African American majority voting districts.

The Supreme Court, as well as the conservative intellectuals in question, have repeatedly cited Supreme Court Justice Harlan's dissenting opinion in the *Plessy v. Ferguson* case as the authoritative statement on the "color-blind" constitution. In this case in 1896, the majority of the Court ruled that "separate but equal" facilities were constitutional, thus permitting "racial" segregation. In his dissent, Harlan said, "Our constitution is color-blind and neither knows nor tolerates class among citizens" and he went on to say that the law "takes no account of" color (Harlan cited in Hofstader 1982:58).

Those who have quoted Harlan, however, have failed to quote the first part of the paragraph in which he spoke on color blindness. At the beginning of the paragraph, he said:

> The White race deems itself to be the dominant race in this country. And so it is, in prestige, in achievements, in education, in wealth, and in power. So,

I doubt not, it will continue to be for all time, if it remains true to its great heritage and holds fast to the principles of constitutional liberty. (Harlan cited in Hofstader 1982:58)

Justice Harlan tried hard to make the majority of the Court understand that the law and the constitution must remain blind to the existence of "race" because color blindness was the best way to maintain White supremacy.

How can a color-blind constitution insure White dominance? Is not color blindness the opposite of "racism"? This book argues that color blindness is not the opposite of racism, it is another form of racism, just as Harlan suggested. This can only be explained, however, by getting completely outside the conventional liberal-conservative paradigm of "race" relations.

Liberals and conservatives alike subscribe to color blindness as the goal of American race relations. They disagree over the role of government in achieving that goal. Liberals have offered virtually no defense of their color-conscious governmental policies except to say that such policies are needed to achieve the goal of color blindness. In this dispute, the conservatives are essentially correct, the constitution is color-blind and the liberal policies in question are unconstitutional. But what the conservatives have done in their attack on liberalism is to inadvertently expose the racism inherent in the constitution.

This book explains just how the constitution is "racist" and how color blindness is actually a racist ideology. Race relations, from the colonial period to the present day, are examined from a historical perspective.

The material conditions that gave rise to a sequence of racist ideologies are analyzed. In addition, this book examines how the "race" problem has been used to the disadvantage of both African American and White working people from the beginning of the country to the present time.

Today there is a renewed interest in race theory because the liberal "color-blind" perspective breaks down under the conservative "color-blind" attack. There is also widespread disillusionment among liberals with existing policies, which were once believed to be solutions to the race problem. President Clinton has declared himself a "New Democrat" and has adopted many of the professed policies of the Republican party, including attacks on affirmative action and welfare.

Despite the gains of African Americans, new problems have emerged and some old, fundamental problems appear to be intractable. Residential segregation of African Americans is still the rule, even in the suburbs (Massey and Denton 1993). Income inequality has increased dramatically within the African American population (Hacker 1995). Research shows that many African Americans in "integrated" occupations are disillusioned because they continue to experience racism despite their success (Feagin and Sikes 1994). My recent research suggests that the majority of African Americans may not subscribe to color-blind ideology at all (Chapter 8, this volume).

One out of three African American men between the ages of 18 and 27 are under the control of the criminal justice system, in jail, or on probation or parole (Hacker 1995). This year, chain gangs have been revived and the use of the death penalty has been expedited. Right-wing militia groups are flourishing and Ku Klux Klan members have been arrested for burning churches in the South. The welfare system has been "reformed" in draconian fashion and highly punitive measures have been taken against immigrants.

Since the 1980s, the rich in this country have increased their wealth in spectacular fashion whereas the income of working people has gone down. "Downsizing" in public and private employment has cost millions of people their jobs. The anger and fear of White Americans, however, has not been directed against the rich or the government but against African Americans, immigrants, affirmative action, welfare, and so forth. There is nothing new in this.

When racism is placed in a historic perspective, it becomes clear that it is not some flaw that impedes the perfection of the American system. Racism was a basic part of the system from the beginning. "Color-blindness" is simply the latest manifestation of it.

REFERENCES

Feagin, Joe and Melvin P. Sikes. 1994. *Living with Racism: The Black Middle-Class Experience*. Boston: Beacon.

Hacker, Andrew. 1995. *Two Nations: Black and White, Separate, Hostile, and Unequal*. New York: Ballantine.

Hofstader, Ralph. 1982. *Great Issues in American History*. New York: Vintage.

Massey, Douglas S. and Nancy A. Denton. 1993. *American Apartheid*. Cambridge, MA: Harvard University Press.

ACKNOWLEDGMENTS

I would like to thank the following people for their help on various aspects of this book. Janice Kohl, Reuben Cooper, Andy Pyle, Gary Waller, Janet Waller, Mona Danner, Carol Seyfrit, Fred Pincus, and Austin Jersild reviewed various chapters. Terry Jones and Bette Dickerson reviewed the prospectus for Sage Publications and three anonymous people reviewed the manuscript—they all made helpful suggestions. I was also assisted by the Honors College at Old Dominion University, graduate assistants Lisa Coffman, Catherine Drezak, and Tony Luckman, and the students in my sociology honors class in the spring of 1992.

1

THEORIES OF IDEOLOGY

Did slavery exist because slave owners distorted Christianity? Did slavery end because Christians eventually discovered slavery to be a sin? Was the postslavery oppression of the sharecropper the result of the belief that African Americans were innately inferior? Did it end because this was discovered to be untrue? Is prejudice the cause of the continuing oppression of African Americans today?

The most important issue in the study of "racist" ideology is whether racist ideas determine "racial" oppression or whether the structures of oppression determine racist ideas. Marx's theory of ideology clearly says that it is the latter but there are other theories of ideology that disagree with this.

Theories of ideology are of three types—Marxist, anti-Marxist, and semi-Marxist. Marx and Engels pioneered the study of ideology in the mid-19th century. Their theory of ideology cannot be separated from their general theory of society. For Marx and Engels, ideology is just one of many parts of what they called the "superstructure" of society. They argued that all the parts of the superstructure, including ideologies such as racist beliefs, are determined by the material "base" of society. Anti-Marxist theories of ideology are based on the inversion of the Marxian argument: The elements of the superstructure are to some degree independent of the elements of the base of society. So, to some extent, ideology can autonomously determine the elements in the base of society. Such a view is called "idealist" in contrast to Marx who is called a "materialist." Some anti-Marxists doubt that the superstructure or the base actually exist so any part

1

can more or less determine any other part of society. Semi-Marxist theories of ideology incorporate a few of Marx's observations about ideology but do not connect them to Marx's general theory.

MARX'S THEORY

In 1859, about midway in Marx's career, Marx and Engels summarized a number of the key features of their theory of society in the often quoted Preface to *A Contribution to the Critique of Political Economy.* Marx's brief summary in the Preface necessarily leaves out many important details and issues. The following discussion takes the key topics as they are presented in the Preface and draws on other works of Marx as well as latter-day theorists to flesh out the theory and examine some of the controversies that surround it.

Beginning with *the base* or foundation of society, Marx and Engels (Preface in Mills 1966) wrote the following:

> In the social production that men carry on they enter into definite relations that are indispensable and independent of their will; these relations of production correspond to a definite stage of development of their material powers of production. The totality of these relations of production constitutes the economic structure of society—the real foundation. (P. 42)

The relations of production, then, are the social relations through which humans organize production in various types of societies. For example, in capitalism the relation of capitalists to workers is an antagonistic wage-labor relationship whereas in hunting and gathering societies there is a nonantagonistic division of labor by gender and age. The material powers of production or the means of production refer to the technology available in a particular society. Together, the means and relations of production are the determining foundation or base of human societies. These two things have a correspondence. Thus, you do not find an advanced relations of production (complex class structure) in a society with a primitive means of production.

Although the means and relations of production correspond, there is a dialectical relationship between them. Marx's dialectical perception of human societies is quite different from the conventional view in which a cause is seen as entirely independent, external, and occurring in time before its effect. Speaking generally of dialectics, Marx explained, "What constitutes *dialectical* movement is the coexistence of two contradictory sides, their conflict and their fusion in a new category" (Marx quoted in Easton and Guddat 1967:483). Thus, things do not exist in isolation, a cause here an effect there. Rather, they exist together in continuous contradiction and it is the contradiction that provides continuous motion to human societies. Society, then, develops in stages out of itself as the result of its own internal contradictions.

Marx and Engels wrote in the Preface (quoted in Mills 1966):

> At a certain stage of development, the material forces of production in society come in conflict with the existing relations of production. . . . From forms of development of the forces of production these relations turn into their fetters. (P. 42)

So, although the relations of production bring about development in the means of production, at some point they block it. In the case of feudalism, whereas feudal relations of production allowed the development of capitalism within it, at a certain point, they blocked further development, which led to the revolutionary overthrow of the ruling class of feudalism, the monarchy, the nobility, and the church. About capitalism, Marx wrote in *Capital I* (quoted in Bottomore 1964):

> Modern industry never looks upon or treats the existing form of a production process as final. The technical basis of industry is therefore revolutionary, while all earlier modes of production were essentially conservative. (P. 252)

Marx did not take technological change as an independent causal factor, this would be faulted as technological determinism. Technological change was seen in terms of its dialectical relationship to the capitalist relations of production. Because of the competitive nature of capitalist production, the capitalist is compelled to constantly improve the means of production (technology) to reduce labor costs and increase profits.

Marx and Engels (quoted in Mills 1966) went on to say in the Preface that the economic base of society is the foundation

> on which legal and political *superstructures* arise and to which definite forms of social consciousness correspond. The mode of production of material life *determines* the general character of the social, political, and spiritual processes of life. It is not the consciousness of men that determines their being, but, on the contrary, their social being determines their consciousness. (P. 42, emphasis added)

Here Marx and Engels clearly placed law and politics and a corresponding social consciousness and social, political, and spiritual processes in the superstructure, which is determined by the base. He later added such things as the state, religion, philosophy, political economy, the military, and so forth to the superstructure.

When the relations of production become absolute fetters on the further development of the means of production:

> Then comes the period of social revolution. With the change of the economic foundation, the entire immense superstructure is more or less rapidly transformed. In considering these transformations the distinction should always be made between the material transformation of the economic conditions of production, which can be determined with the precision of the natural science, and the legal, political, religious, esthetic, or philosophic—in short the *ideological forms* in which men become conscious of this conflict and fight it out. (Preface quoted in Mills 1966:42-3)

The contradictions in the base are finally resolved by revolution and in the process, a new superstructure is created. Participants, however, do see the process in this way but in an ideological way. In the transition to capitalism, for example, the capitalist class constructed a new superstructure for the purpose of defending the new structure of inequality in the base, but expressed what it was doing in terms such as "liberty," "equality," and "democracy."

Historically, ideology began when societies developed classes and priests become part of the class which no longer engaged in productive activity.

> From this moment on consciousness can really boast of being something other than consciousness of existing practice, of *really* representing something without representing something real. From this moment on consciousness can emancipate itself from the world and proceed to the formation of "pure" theory, theology, philosophy, ethics, etc. (Marx quoted in Easton and Guddat 1967:422-3)

Early humans were conscious of nature, which they worshipped and, "which appears to man as an entirely alien, omnipotent, and unassailable force" (Marx quoted in Easton and Guddat 1967:422). As the division of labor advanced, humans gained more control over nature. But in this process society was partitioned into individual families opposing one another. The nucleus of property was in the family "where wife and children are the slaves of man" (Marx quote in Easton and Guddat 1967:424). Religion changed in this process. Priests now existed along side a ruling class. Thus it was that society replaced nature as an alien, omnipotent, and an unassailable force. It became the role of religion to hide the truth of the world, the existence of classes and their essential contradictions, which compose an inverted world in which those disconnected from real, material production rule the rest. But phantoms, the mental inventions of priests, are declared to rule the world:

> Religious suffering is the expression of real suffering and at the same time the protest against real suffering. Religion is the sigh of the oppressed creature, the heart of a heartless world, as it is the spirit of spiritless conditions. It is the opium of the people. . . . Religion is only the illusory sun that revolves around man so long as he does not revolve about himself. (Marx quoted in Easton and Guddat 1967:250-1)

Man makes religion, religion does not make man, but this truth, along with many others, is inverted in religious consciousness.

With the development of capitalism, a critique of religion became possible. But the development of capitalism does not end religion, it transformed it and revitalized it. In addition, in capitalism a vast entourage of professional ideologists pick up the prejudices of the bourgeois class and transform them into social and economic "theory." These ideologists, like their nonproductive priestly counterparts, believe that ideas determine the world.

Ideology makes the world a mystery, an overwhelming and incomprehensible thing and this, in turn, promotes dependence, apathy, and resignation. One of the critical things that ideology does to mystify the world is to hide, deny, and especially invert contradictions (Larrain 1983).

Ideology directs people toward ineffective solutions. It "sublimates," diverting energy into "socially acceptable" substitutes for real transformations. It solves contradictions in imagination that cannot be solved in the real world. In these ways, ideology preserves inequality and protects the primary contradictions in the base of society and thus serves the ruling class. To use an analogy, ideology is like the oil in an internal combustion engine. The oil greatly extends the time over which an engine destroys itself. Marx argued that criticism cannot destroy an ideology. Rather, it is finally abolished when the material base with which it is associated is abolished.

Larrain (1983) notes that Marx and Engels never used the term *ideology* to refer to its opposite, which is critical, negative theory. Lenin did do this, however, probably because he did not have access to Marx's early works (Larrain 1983). For example, in *What Is to Be Done?,* Lenin (1973) frequently referred to "socialist ideology." Thus, ideology was a matter of class position—different classes have different ideologies. But Marx did not argue that all thought in the bourgeois class was completely ideological. He often acknowledged the important insights of certain bourgeois philosophers and political economists. Workers were not necessarily revolutionary either. Larrain (1983) argues that, for Marx, ideological thought is a matter of not grasping contradictions. Perhaps, for the sake of clarity, analysis that does grasp contradictions should be called *counter-ideology.*

In *Das Kapital,* Marx's most important work, his objective was a comprehensive analysis of capitalist economy. Nevertheless, he returned to the question of ideology on a number of occasions in these works. Capitalist ideology makes many claims about freedom, individuality, rights of humankind, democracy, and so forth. Yet capitalism is composed of classes exhibiting great extremes of inequality. For Marx, these claims, then, must be ideologies and as such they must be reflecting the actual, inverted structure of capitalist society. Marx's critique of the capitalist "marketplace" turns out to be a particularly important one for the study of color-blind racist ideology because "color blindness" is actually derived from the classic notions of bourgeois freedom and individuality. Marx argued in *Capital I* that commodity production gives rise to the notion of an abstract "man" and his rights.

Marx (quoted in Bottomore 1983) wrote the following:

> The sphere of circulation or commodity exchange within whose boundaries the sale and purchase of labor-power goes on, is in fact a very Eden of the innate rights of man. It is the exclusive realm of Freedom, Equality, Property, and Bentham. Freedom, because both buyer and seller of a commodity, let us say of labor-power, are determined by their own free will. They contract as free persons, who are equal before the law. Their contract is the final result in which their joint will finds a common legal expression. Equality, because each enters into relations with the other, as with a simple owner of commodities, and they exchange equivalent for equivalent. Property, because each disposes only of what is his own. And Bentham, because each looks only to his own advantage. (P. 156)

People in general see a process of free exchange of labor, wages, and commodities in the marketplace. Political economists also see a process of free exchange. Marx, argues that, on one hand, it is a free exchange. The market is real and the market is the main arena in which men and women can realize the freedom that does exist, to the extent that it does exist, in capitalism. In this form, then, "man" is "free" and declared free. On the other hand, it is precisely in this exchange that classes are produced and reproduced and "man" is not free. The way in which labor is made abstract in capitalism gives rise to the ideology of the free man, the individual abstracted so to speak from society itself.

In capitalism the worker "freely" sells his or her labor power in the marketplace of employment. It takes living workers to bring labor power to the marketplace. The cost of living workers is determined by what it costs to create and maintain them and enable them to reproduce. That cost varies from place to place and these variations are averaged out in the labor marketplace. So, wages are paid according to the average cost of bringing various workers alive into the marketplace and maintaining them at various levels of existence. Within the logic of capitalism, then, the wages paid are fair wages.

Capitalists then have those living persons for a specified number of hours each day to labor according to their direction. It is the intention and the absolute necessity of capitalists as a class to sell their products for more than the wages that they pay to workers as a class. The difference between all the wages paid and the value of all the commodities sold is called *surplus value*. Surplus value is the source of all capital, as such it is the essence of capitalism. Looking at an individual worker, it can be explained as follows. During part of the time that workers work, they create the value that is the value of their wages. In the remaining time, workers create surplus value, which will go to the capitalist. This value is not realized, however, until the commodity is sold in the marketplace. For commodities to be exchanged at all they must have something in common on which an exchange value can be calculated. This value cannot be use value, which is the actual use that each commodity has for each particular consumer, because use value is particular to the individual and not a common value. The only thing that all commodities have in common is labor. Commodities have a value that is determined by the socially necessary labor time needed to produce them. *Socially* refers to the averaging process that occurs when commodities in general enter the marketplace. This is what Marx means by "homogeneous human labor." Capitalists do not realize surplus value until their commodities encounter homogeneous human labor in the marketplace.

The bourgeois political economist, having discovered that the value of labor is related to the value of commodities, seems to believe that the exchange value of commodities consists of the exchange value of labor—wages. If this were true, there would be no surplus value. The cost of commodities must include surplus value, the value created by the worker but appropriated by the capitalist when commodities are equated. Here we see the inescapable and fundamental contradiction between capital and labor, surplus value against wages. Among other things, this contradiction produces the "business cycle." How can workers as a class, the majority of the population, consume the goods that are produced if their wages cannot equal the value of the goods? The answer is sometimes they can and sometimes they cannot. They can during the giddy expansionist "growth" phase of capitalism when capital is accumulated. But this phase is always haunted by the ghost of contraction, "recession" or "depression." Capitalism has two inherent tendencies, infinite expansion and infinite contraction. Thus, the "business cycle" expresses the elementary contradictions of capitalism.

Before capitalism, theorists were completely mystified by commodities and their exchange. Marx wrote the following (quoted in Bottomore 1964):

It was, however, impossible for Aristotle to discover from the form of value itself that in the form of commodity values all labor is expressed as equivalent human labor, and consequently as *labor of equal worth.* Greek society was founded upon slavery, and had, therefore, for its natural basis, the inequality of men and of their labor powers. The secret of the expression of value, namely, that *all kinds of labor are equal and equivalent* because so far as they are human labor in general, cannot be deciphered until the notion of human equality has already acquired the fixity of a popular prejudice. (P. 86, emphasis added)

Capitalism is the first form of society in which the notion of human equality becomes a popular prejudice. With capitalism there is a great popular cry for freedom, liberty, equality, rights, and so forth. This is a result of the form of society at this stage of development. Specifically, the form is the "marketplace" in which commodities are apparently freely exchanged, workers selling labor power, capitalists selling commodities. Within this form is hidden a truth—the labor of all people is equal. But this truth cannot be realized in this form. Nevertheless, this form inspired bourgeois ideologists to declare that the equality of "man" had arrived. For Marx, the bourgeois political economists discovered much about the operations of capitalism, but because of their material limitations they could not get to the essence of capitalism. They accepted the existing form of capitalism as immortal.

Thus, the bourgeois economist knows that the value of labor is related to the exchange of commodities but cannot see the implication of what it means that commodities are equated in this way. What it means is that all people really are equal and it is the value of their equal labor that makes them equal. To put it another way, all the labor that makes society possible is of equal value, the labor of garbage collector and the labor of the scientist. But the capitalist world must exist infused with extreme inequality. Commodities are not exchanged on the basis of equally valued human labor, but on the basis of labor as a commodity and surplus value. How could the ideologist reconcile the sense of liberty with the reality of extreme inequality? The bourgeois political economist simply saw "man" free in the marketplace and declared "man" free.

The political ideologists who wrote the *Constitution of the United States* made "man" free this way. Then, as now, one finds only free individuals before the law. There are no classes, genders, slaves, Native American nations, or African American people before the law. This legal "Eden," as Marx called it, is an exact inversion of the real world and an absolute denial of the existence of the most elementary contradictions of this society. It is an ideological statement. "Color blindness" is simply one of those ideologies that can be derived from such a constitution.

ANTI-MARXIAN THEORIES OF IDEOLOGY

Despite the fact that Marx wrote over and over that the base of society determines the superstructure, legions of theorists, many calling themselves "Marxists," have tried to make determination, in some way, go from superstructure to base.

For example, French Marxist structuralism argues that elements that Marx placed in the superstructure have "relative autonomy." Miles (1982), a present-day structuralist, would avoid any "economic determinism" in Marx by arguing that ideology has "relative autonomy." Against this one must ask, to the extent that things in the superstructure are autonomous, what determines them? Among the many other criticisms of this structuralism is that it is a static, nondialectical, functional view in which structures become deterministic (Ritzer 1988:142-53).

Max Weber, not a Marxist, wrote at the end of *The Protestant Ethic and Spirit of Capitalism* that "it is, of course, not my aim to substitute for a one-sided materialistic an equally one-sided spiritualistic causal interpretation of culture and of history. *Each is equally possible* (Weber quoted in Zeitlin 1994:171, emphasis added). For Weber, determination can go either way, from economic activity to religion or vice versa. It was a matter of investigation. Mommsen (1985:235) notes that "Weber took exception, above all else to the Marxist theory of the 'superstructure.' "

If the parts of society do not have some predictable, determinant relationship to each other, as these anti-Marxists argue, no theory of society is possible. From this standpoint, it would seem that even Marx's critics would have to concede that his theory has the virtue of actually being a theory.

There is a classic, political issue associated with this debate over the relationship of the base and superstructure. Marx's analysis implies that reformist efforts that "work through the system" cannot achieve an equalitarian society. A revolution is needed because the ruling class has created the dominating elements of the superstructure ("the system") and can ultimately control all the elements in the superstructure to preserve the inegalitarian relations of production in the base. Reformers argue that inequality can be ameliorated or perhaps entirely overcome by such things as political activity, religious appeals, values, education, legal action, and so forth. Such things can even bring on revolutionary change, it is sometimes argued.

Marx noted that people often see elements in the superstructure appearing to determine the base because they take a perspective that is too limited. He wrote in *The German Ideology* (quoted in Easton and Guddat 1967):

This contradiction between the productive forces and the form of commerce, which we observe occurring several times in past history without endangering the basis of history, had to burst out in a revolution each time, taking on at the same time various *secondary* forms, such as comprehensive collisions, collisions of various classes, contradictions of consciousness, battle of ideas, etc., political struggle, etc. *From a narrow point of view* one can isolate one of these secondary forms and consider it the basis of the revolutions. This is all the more easy as the individuals who started the revolutions had illusions about their own activity. (P. 454, emphasis added)

Marx, of course, argued that when revolutionary conditions do develop, a conscious, revolutionary force is needed to produce the desired outcome.

SEMI-MARXIAN THEORIES OF IDEOLOGY

Almost universally in the social sciences, and in general discourse as well, "ideology" has been stripped of most of what Marx meant by the concept. Ideology has been made to refer to belief systems that different classes have that are related to their interests. Ideology justifies these interests. Macionis (1995:249), for example, defines ideology as "cultural beliefs that, directly or indirectly, justify social stratification."

With such definitions, all the following are lost: base and superstructure and their relationship, the role of ideologists and their connection to the ruling class, the material origins of ideology, contradiction, the inversion or denial of contradiction, the difference between the oppressed and the oppressor, and the difference between ideology and counterideology. In this way, just as his theory predicts, Marx's theory of ideology has been made into an ideology.

SUMMARY

In short, Marx's theory argues that the elements of the superstructure exist to preserve the structure of inequality in the base of society. They are controlled by the ruling class to contain the contradictory forces that threaten to overthrow the existing system. At some point, however, the contradictions within the base cannot be contained and new structures emerge in the base, which then requires a transformed superstructure. Thus, the progression of racist ideology in this country from its Christian form to its evolutionary form to the current "color-blind" form can be understood as the consequence of changes that have occured in the means and relations of production. If, however, a narrow, limited view is taken, it will appear that changes in racist ideas along with other elements in the superstructure have brought about changes in racial oppression.

REFERENCES

Bottomore, T. B. 1964. *Karl Marx.* New York: McGraw-Hill.
Bottomore, Tom, ed. 1983. *A Dictionary of Marxist Thought.* Cambridge, MA: Harvard University Press.
Easton, Lloyd and Kurt Guddat. 1967. *Writings of the Young Marx on Philosophy and Society.* Garden City, NY: Doubleday.

Larrain, Jorge. 1983. *Marxism and Ideology.* Atlantic Highlands, NJ: Humanities Press.

Lenin, V. I. 1973. *What Is to Be Done?* Peking, China: Peking Foreign Languages Press.

Macionis, John J. 1995. *Sociology.* New York: Prentice Hall.

Miles, Robert. 1982. *Racism and Migrant Labor.* London, England: Routledge.

Mills, C. Wright. 1966. *The Marxists.* New York: Dell.

Mommsen, W. J. 1985. "Capitalism and Socialism: Weber's Dialogue with Marx." Pp. 234-73 in *A Weber-Marx Dialogue,* edited by R. Antonio and R. Glassman. Lawrence: University of Kansas Press.

Ritzer, George. 1988. *Contemporary Sociological Theory.* 2d ed. New York: Knopf.

Zeitlin, Irving M. 1994. *Ideology and the Development of Sociological Theory.* New Jersey: Prentice Hall.

2

CHRISTIANITY, THE CONSTITUTION, AND SLAVERY

Why was slave labor employed in colonial America? Why was the labor force split along "racial" lines? What did African Americans become after two and a half centuries in America? Why did the Civil War occur? These questions are addressed in this chapter from a materialist perspective while the accommodation of Christianity and the constitution to slavery is examined as an ideological phenomenon.

WHY SLAVERY?

Franklin Frazier (1957) observed that forced labor was the hallmark of the colonized world. Frazier wrote the following:

> Slavery has developed in those areas with "open resources," which are defined as those areas in which "everyone who is able-bodied and not defective in mind can provide for himself independently of any capitalist or landlord." Hence, to secure a cheap and disciplined labor supply for capitalistic exploitation, it has been necessary to create a system of forced labor. . . . A characteristic of the plantation institution is a labor problem, which everywhere tends to be defined also as a race problem. (Pp. 111-12)

In the 17th century, England was the most advanced capitalist country in the world and it was in the North American colonies that English capitalism was the least restrained (Elkins 1968). Here, a new type of society could be created with only limited controls from King, Parliament, church, or "feudal immunities." There were great risks but also great opportunities for investors in North America to take land, clear it, and produce crops for export into the developing world system of trade. But how could the necessary labor force be obtained? Experiments with enslaving Native Americans were not at all promising. Such activity could set off deadly attacks from Native American nations and slaves could flee into a country they knew. Enslavement of English people had been abolished in England centuries earlier. It would have been a tricky matter to attempt to enslave English immigrants once in the New World because word of this would have undermined the attempts to lure immigrants to the colonies. Unfree labor in the form of indentured servitude and convict labor were therefore employed extensively. Indentured servants were bought, sold, and treated much like slaves. But their tenure was only five to seven years and if land was available for subsistence farming, those free of indenture, and immigrants as well, were not much interested in plantation labor at low wages especially in the torrid and disease-ridden coastal areas of the South.

MULTINATIONAL UPRISINGS

While the condition of slaves was clearly the worst throughout the colonies, that of indentured Whites was hardly better, and the majority of free Whites lived in extreme poverty (Fresia 1988). In colonies like Virginia, the planter class, with huge land grants, stood high above all the common people. In the mid-17th century the Virginia Assembly invented ways to extend the terms of servitude while the planter class accumulated uncultivated lands to restrict the options of the free worker (Morgan 1975). These class contradictions produced a series of small uprisings in the southern colonies until there was a major explosion in Virginia in 1676 in what was known as "Bacon's Rebellion." The governor was forced to flee the burning capital of Jamestown as the uprising spread across the whole colony. England had to send soldiers on war ships to put down what was actually an attempt at revolution (Fresia 1988). The events in Jamestown were viewed with great alarm by the propertied class throughout the colonies because it involved slaves, indentured servants, and poor Whites who had united under the leadership of Nathaniel Bacon, a property owner who initially wanted to seize Native American lands. When the planter class would not provide militia support for this, he attacked them, their homes, and other property. The event was seen by the planters as springing from "hopes of leveling" among those without property (Zinn 1995:42). According to Allen (1994), "the main rebel force came to be made up of Anglo- and African American bond laborers together demanding an end to bond servitude." As his forces grew, Bacon openly condemned the rich for their oppression of the poor (Breen 1973). This attempt at revolution was put down by force and false promises of amnesty and ended with a number of people being hanged.

THE ORIGINS OF THE "RACE" PROBLEM

Several more uprisings of this type followed that of Bacon but fateful steps were taken by the planters to transform the existing class contradictions into another form. The planters decided to greatly increase the importing of slaves, to reduce the number of indentured servants, and to be much more selective in choosing them. Indenture virtually ended by the turn of the century. Slaves, who made up 8 percent of the total population in 1690, were 21 percent of the total in 1770 (Fresia 1988). Instead of English-speaking, "seasoned" slaves being imported mainly from the West Indies, many more slaves were shipped directly from Africa. In addition, White settlers were allowed much greater access to Native American lands. And there was a deliberate extension of special privileges to all Whites to drive a wedge between them and the slaves (Morgan 1975). For example, indentured servants were allowed to join militias and slave patrols (Zinn 1995:56). Most important, barriers were created so that free labor would not be placed in competition with slave labor. In this way, White workers gained the opportunity to bargain for better conditions for themselves after planters saw the consequences of bringing the condition of propertyless Whites down near the level of slaves.

No doubt the colonial rulers would have preferred to keep White labor near the level of slaves but the fact was that they often lost control of the systems of inequality that they had created. During the last quarter of the 17th century, a variety of militant confrontations brought down the established governments of Massachusetts, New York, Maryland, Virginia, and North Carolina. By 1760, there had been 18 rebellions aimed at overthrowing colonial governments, 6 African American rebellions, and 40 major riots protesting a variety of unfair conditions (Fresia 1988:27).

WHITE WORKERS DEFEND THEIR WAGES

It is clear that White workers defended and expanded their privileges. The development of a system whereby both slaves and free African American people came to be excluded from White occupations must be understood in this light. As early as 1686 in New York city, slaves and free African American people were prohibited from working as porters (Zinn 1995:57). In 1768 in Charlestown, Massachusetts, working people demanded that merchants stop importing slaves who were being hired out as crafts people. When their demands were not met, they ignored the existing property qualifications to vote, voted in their own General Assembly, and took control of the city government (Fresia 1988:29). In 1793, cordwainers and master tailors in Charleston published at their own expense the ordinances banning slaves from their trades (Jordon 1969:406). Virginia set limits as to the number of slaves that could be employed on water craft and Maryland and North Carolina forbid the hiring out of slaves (Jordon 1969:406). These same forces lead to greater restrictions on manumission, release from slavery. When slavery was ended in Pennsylvania in the early 1800s, African American people were driven out of the skilled trades in Philadelphia (Du Bois 1967:33).

So, it is clear that in the colonial period there was no race prejudice strong enough to prevent Whites and African Americans from uniting at times to try to overthrow the ruling class. Such "prejudice" arose after enslaving elites split the labor force. Then White workers responded to the logic of the situation to preserve and expand their "racially" privileged position.

THE AFRICAN AMERICAN ANTI-NATION

Slaves were defined in law in terms of what they could not be. The essence of this definition was in the property relationship. The free White person had the right to own property and buy and sell labor power and accumulate whatever wealth might accumulate from these transactions. The slave was property. For a time, he or she was defined as real property, attached to the land in feudal fashion but this impeded sale and inheritance of slaves so the slave was made personal property, chattel. Elkins (1968:59) cites a 19th century judge who said, "A slave is in absolute bondage; he has no civil right, and can hold no property, except at the will and pleasure of his master." Elkins goes on to say the following:

(The slave) could neither give nor receive gifts; he could make no will, nor could he by will, inherit anything. He could not hire himself out or make contracts for any purpose . . . and thus neither his word nor his bond had any standing in law. He could buy or sell nothing at all, except as his master's agent, could keep no cattle, horses, hogs or sheep and, in Mississippi at least, could raise no cotton. Even masters who permitted such transactions, except under express arrangement, were uniformly liable to fines. (P. 59)

Thus, we see the extraordinary thing that the planter class wished to create. These people would have no economy of their own and no way of developing an economy of their own. They would be totally without property and could not retain any of the wealth that they created through their own labor. African American people would live but they would not live on any land that was their own. They could never be part of a nation or form a nation themselves because they were to exist without any economic base. They would have neither a means of production nor a relations of production of their own.

As for superstructure, whereas White people had legal marriage and descent was patrilineal, African American people could not marry and descent was made matrilineal. There were no "legitimate children." There were no legal African American fathers or mothers. One would think there was no African American family. African American women gave birth to slaves, the property of their slave masters. Who the father was, African American or White, had no bearing on the matter. Thus, the capital invested in slaves could reproduce itself many times over and slavery was made hereditary and perpetual. Similarly, manumission from slavery was taxed and impeded at every turn.

Planters feared any kind of slave assembly and made it illegal. On their own plantations, some planters allowed slaves to hear White preachers but African American preachers were illegal. Slaves could not leave their plantations without passes. Their world was to be the plantation. It was illegal to teach slaves to read or write so they were to be without such knowledge. African culture and language was suppressed. The African American person had no protection of law. They could only testify against another African American person. Essentially, the slave master was the law on his own plantation. The cruelest corporal punishment was legal and the life of a slave could be taken with impunity.

This, then, was the African American *anti-nation*. The planter class designed in law a thing in which living people would exist without a base or superstructure. People would live as "atoms" outside of society. But, as

Marx argued, law is only a part of the superstructure. The dominant force in the base writes the law but the base has within it two contradictory sides, in this case, an African American side as well as a White side. Both sides, and the struggle between them, determined social reality.

THE AFRICAN AMERICAN NATION

As White people formed a new nation in North America, African American people did the same. By the time of the Civil War, 4,000,000 slaves lived in the slave states. Clearly, it is not possible for such a number of people to exist for two and a half centuries excluded from White society without forming a society of their own. From the beginning to the end, slave life never conformed to the fantasy of the planter as it was expressed in law. From the beginning, African American people drew themselves together in solidarity, and, as best they could, manipulated, resisted, sabotaged, and rebelled against the repressive system of the ruling class of the White nation. The anti-nation was the fantasy of the planter class. For language, African American people, like White people, created a dialect within the English language. Most African American people adopted Christianity to their needs and, despite the attempts to prevent it, they often had African American preachers. They married, were faithful, had enduring kinship networks, and resisted forced marriages (Gutman 1977).

Bennett (1982) notes that Du Bois traced the founding of the African American nation to the North when, in 1787, eight free men in Philadelphia drew up a social compact called the Free Africa Society. Du Bois called it "the first wavering step of a people toward organized social life" (Bennett 1982:56). Similar societies were founded in Boston, New York, and Newport, Rhode Island. These societies were followed by the beginning of an African American church movement, a lodge movement, and the start of African American schools. Politically, slavery was challenged in the courts as early as 1766 and with mass pressure in the form of meetings, petitions, and legislative pleas (Bennett 1982:58).

Especially in the South, the White nation lived in mortal fear of what it had created. The law charged all White people with the responsibility of repressing African American people. Whites were punished for not upholding the so-called Black Codes. Whites were formed into patrols to watch for the movement of African American people without passes. Militias were used to deal with any sign of rebellion. But none of this really calmed White fears. Stories spread far and wide, some true some not, of slaves poisoning their masters, of slaves attacking or killing them, and of collective African American uprisings.

Aptheker (1969) has documented many instances in which both small and large bands of armed, runaway slaves lived in desolate areas, raided White farms, and fought against troops hunting for them. Some runaways found sanctuary within Native American nations although Native Americans sometimes hunted them down for White owners. Eventually, there was an effective "underground railway." Of course, there were actual slave uprisings like that lead by Gabriel and Nat Turner.[1] Many slaves were able to negotiate the purchase of their freedom with their own labor and free African American people bought the freedom of other family members. In these matters, some judges were remarkably sympathetic to slaves. From the beginning, and in increasing numbers, White and African American abolitionists wrote and spoke against slavery and, in a few instances, lead insurrections against it.

CHRISTIAN RACIST IDEOLOGY

In the colonial period, racist ideology was primarily religious in form. It was said that African people were the descendants of Ham, the son of Noah. In Genesis, it is said that Noah cursed Ham because he looked on his father's nakedness. The curse was that he would become a servant for life. But there is nothing at all that suggests that Ham was Black. Jordon (1969) said that such a link was made in the Jewish Talmud, part of the curse was being turned black. Just how this might have become part of Christian thinking is not at all clear (Jordon 1969). Nevertheless, Christians found that the Bible sanctioned the system of slavery that they were creating.

This theological racism can be understood along the lines suggested by both Durkheim and Marx. Religion mystifies the real, material, social world. "God" is the real force of society in mystified form. In this case, African people were said by Whites to be cursed by God, made into slaves by God, blackened by God and they existed outside the Kingdom of God, which is White. Demystified, this simply means that the African was cursed by Whites, enslaved by Whites, and could never be a recognized part of the White nation. They could never be a recognized part of the White nation because they were an indispensable part, the heritable slave part, of the system of labor existing at that time. These were the facts of their actual condition. The planters explained the real world by employing a racist theology. God created the African American slave and free White people, they preached. This inverts what happened, enslaving White elites created, themselves, the African American slave, the White worker, and a racist God. Thus, Christianity, as ideology, was used to explain the material world as being constructed by a supernatural force instead of the planter class.

In the earliest colonial period, there was confusion whether slaves who were already Christian when imported from the Caribbean could be held as slaves. Traditionally, Christians enslaved non-Christians. Thus, the category "Christian" is often found in the writing of the early law where one expects to see "White." The same confusion arose with regards to those slaves who became Christians in America. It was argued that slaves could not become Christians because Christians did not enslave each other (Klein 1967). The problem was simply solved by making religious status irrelevant to slave status. Being an African Black person was the defining criteria, Christian or not. Just as Ham was made Black when he was not, the Christian justification for enslavement, being non-Christian, was redefined by Christians to being Black.

Very early on, marital and sexual relations between African American and White people were condemned and then outlawed. A law created in Maryland in 1681 characterized such marriages as a "disgrace not only of the English but also of many other Christian nations (Jordon 1969:79-80). It was "un-Christian" for Whites to marry African American people. Demystified, the problem with interracial marriages was that it would undermine slavery. The offspring of White fathers would have legally been free. If intermarried, African American people could have inherited White land and slaves. Kin would be oppressing kin. The law was clear, there would be no intermarriage despite the intermixing that occurred.

FROM BLACK NATION TO BLACK "RACE," A QUESTION OF IDEOLOGY

In the 17th and 18th century, the term *nation* was used much more broadly than it is today. For example, nation referred to European peoples like the English, Welsh, Irish, and so forth and it referred to the "Indians" as a nation and to specific Native American nations. It was also common to refer to the "Negro" or "Black" nation. Significantly, this latter practice seems to have stopped in the years following the American revolution. Thomas Jefferson is something of a transitional figure in this regard. He used both nation and race when referring to African American people in his writings around the end of the 18th century (Jordon 1969). *Race* became the dominant term in the 19th century. Why did race replace nation?

In its Latin origins nation refers to "natio" or birth. It means, more or less, a people associated by birth with a territory (Costello 1995). The term race is of French origins and, at its broadest, simply refers to a category of something, usually people. If people, it refers to a group of people related by common descent (Costello 1995). In the 18th century, race did not yet have the meaning of a genetically determined category of people. Nevertheless, a subtle difference between, nation and race was developing by this time. Nation suggests that the people in question have some form of unifying social organization, that they are a society. Race identifies people more broadly than this. Although they may have a common descent, race does not imply that they, as a people, exist in a common social organization or any social organization.

The switch from nation to race to characterize African American people in North America can only be understood in historic context. Specifically, it occurred as a result of the successful assertion of the White nation in North America of its right to self determination against English rule. *Self-determination* means "the freedom of a people to determine the way in which they shall be governed and whether they shall be self-governed" (Costello 1995).

The American revolution was a dramatic and historic confirmation of a people, a new White nation, to the right of self-determination. That White nation asserted its right to separate from the larger, English society, and to use force to do so. Thus, the American White race was proclaimed a nation by the ruling class that then created a State. African American people were never again to be called a nation but only a race. Races do not have the right of self-determination, nations do. A race became something that was not a nation, had no national existence, and could not possibly have a state. Thus, the term, race, can be seen as a very important ideological part of the effort to define the White-African American political struggle, eliminating one set of possibilities and allowing only certain others. The ruling class of the White nation, with its state in place, ruled African American people who were now called a race. The new American nationalism developed in two dimensions simultaneously, as a nation-state[2] asserting its rights against other nation-states and internally against the development of any such rights for its oppressed races. Defining African American people as a race is entirely consistent with the notion of the African American anti-nation discussed above, the fantasy of the planter class that African American people could be made to exist but not exist as a people. The choice of the term race at this time anticipated the development of the racist ideology that was to come, the argument that African American people were genetically inferior. The theory of evolution and genetics did not yet exist; nevertheless, people like Jefferson speculated that African American people were innately incapable of civilization (Jordon 1969). So, even at this early stage, race, as applied to African American people, carried the notion that here were a people incapable of forming a nation, developing a state, or even participating in such an advanced form of social organization. In short, race, as applied to African American people, is inescapably a racist term, not because it infers innate inferiority but because it substitutes race for nation and thus denies the very existence of African American people as a people, as a nation. It indiscriminately combines African American people with all the "Black" people of the world. This is similar to the way the term *Indian* or *Red man* combined approximately 1,000,000 people living in 600 Native North American nations into one category (Frazier 1957:12).

A related error occurs when a formal definition of a nation is used to judge whether or not an oppressed nation "qualifies" or has the characteristics of a nation. The formal definition is based on the characteristics of free nations, not oppressed nations. The two cannot be equated. An oppressing nation seeks to strip away or prevent the development of the those very things that make up a free nation, such as control of a territory, culture, language, and so forth. (See Carr 1981, for a discussion of Stalin's error in giving a formal definition of nations). An oppressed nation should not be seen in terms of what is, but dialectically, in terms of what is possible given the contradictory forces between the oppressing and the oppressed nation. The characteristics of the African American nation today are discussed in detail in Chapter 8 in terms of territory, political life, economy, class structure, institutions, culture, beliefs, ideology, and oppression.

In political struggle, the strongest possible position is to not even recognize the existence of an adversary. For example, the English were in the habit of referring to the conquered Irish people as a race. Today, England will not talk with the IRA (Irish Republican Army), which is termed a "terrorist" organization. Only recently did Israel talk with the PLO (Palestinian Liberation Organization), which was also referred to as a terrorist organization. The Palestinians are defined as a people without a homeland or a state. The United States would not recognize "Red" China for decades after the revolution in that country. Similarly, at peace talks in Paris at the end of the Vietnam war, U.S. negotiators tried to prevent the NLF (National Liberation Front) from participating. Ultimately, whether a people become a nation or not is a matter of political struggle, never a matter of definition.

Calling a people a race is a way of defining the people in question as beneath political recognition. Race was the term of choice for White nationalists because it defined the contradiction between White and African American in the way that was most advantageous to White. Thus, there was a nation, understood to be White, that had a race problem.

A BLIND CONSTITUTION

In writing the constitution, it was agreed that the question of ending the importing of slaves could not be considered until 1808, fugitive slaves would be returned, and slaves would be counted as three fifths of a person for purposes of (White) representation in Congress. All of this was done in a "color-blind" way, the word "slave" was never used. For example, to specify representation, it was written: "the whole Number of free Persons . . . and three fifths of all other Persons."

One of the founders, James Madison, wrote that it would be "wrong to admit in the constitution that there could be property in men" (Lively 1992:8). Some have suggested that the founders omitted the word slave from the constitution because of guilt (Eastland and Bennett 1979).

It was not a matter of guilt but of ideology. Marx's analysis of bourgeois constitutions is relevant here. Marx noted, for example, that in capitalist society, religion had been banished from the realm of politics. In America, he noted, there was no state religion and political rights were not contingent on any particular religious beliefs. But the result was that religion was "fresh and vital." The state had freed itself from religion but the people had not. Furthermore, the state had abolished as political categories birth, rank, education, occupation, and private property as well. Nevertheless, they all operated vigorously in "civil society," which is to say, the base of society (Marx quoted in Easton and Guddat 1967:223).

In feudalism, classes, "estates," and religion were openly recognized by the state. The feudal state could not stand without being wrapped in religion. In capitalism, however, the state comes into its own, Marx observed.

He expressed both the progress over feudalism and the limitations of the new capitalist society in saying (Marx quoted in Easton and Guddat 1967):

Man [sic] was not freed from religion; he received religious freedom. He was not freed from property. He received freedom of property. He was not freed from the egoism of trade but received freedom to trade. (P. 240)

In capitalism, the new state, like Christianity, ideologically expressed the universal existence of individuals but in a secular way. The American constitution was written to describe a society, Eden, that did not exist and to not describe the society that did exist. Contradictions between classes, European invaders and Native American nations, and slave owners and slaves were all denied by denying the very existence of the categories. In achieving ideological purity, the founding fathers left matters to civil society and to the states to, more or less, do as they wished with regard to the people in these categories. Thus, it could be declared that the country was founded on great ideals, lofty principles, not on the material reality of genocide and slavery. That is why the word slave did not appear in the constitution.

TOWARD CIVIL WAR

The wage labor-slave labor contradiction had, of course, a geographic form. James Madison explained that the main cause of sectional differences was not size, it was "partly from climate, but principally from the effects of their having or not having slaves" (Lively 1992:3). At the time of the Revolution, slavery was well established in five states but it had been abolished or would eventually be abolished in the other eight. But as Madison observed, plantation slavery ended where the climate made it useless. And, of course, where the plantation flourished, antislavery, Christianity, and secular morality withered, an interesting natural experiment that tends to support Marx's argument that the base of society determines the elements in the superstructure such as antislavery values rather than the other way around.

If it is true that at the time of independence there was an assumption that slavery would simply die out, the consequences of the invention of the cotton gin in 1793 must have put an end to that idea. The cotton gin and the power loom greatly reduced the cost of cotton, which led to a boom in cotton production and a boom in the demand for slaves. Federal law forbade Americans to import slaves in 1794, but slave traders of other countries could continue to ply their trade in this country and Americans engaged in illegal slave running anyway. The import of slaves was banned altogether in 1808. But illegal slave running continued and with an ever-expanding slave population, the internal commerce in slaves continued to grow as did the demand for ever more slave territory in what had been Native American lands. Cotton became the country's largest export and American textile mills in the North became the nucleus of the industrial revolution in this country (Foner 1990).

For strategic reasons, England had recognized Native American nations as nations and had restrained the theft of their land. In this regard, the success of the American Revolution was a disaster for the Native American. Critically though, the great land grab that followed the Revolution progressively intensified the slave labor-free labor contradiction in the country. The ideological denial of this contradiction gave way to open political conflict as the struggle to make the new territories either slave labor or free labor states exploded into civil war. Thus, slavery grown large on genocide begat fratricide on a grand scale.

SLAVERY ENDS

The slavery associated with the development of European colonialism generally ended in the 19th century. England, for example, which had bought and sold about 2,000,000 African slaves over the course of two centuries, peacefully ended slavery in 1833. The government provided 20,000,000 pounds to compensate the English slave owners for their loss of property, about 25 pounds per slave. In England, the abolition movement was linked to the ideas of free trade and laissez faire capitalism, which were the doctrines of the ascending industrial capitalist class. Capital now found greater returns in industry than in the plantations. English workers were not threatened by the end of slavery. Slavery had served its purpose, a labor force was in place in the colonies and, after two centuries, slaves had no where to go when they were freed. It was argued that wage labor could replace slavery under these new conditions. It was found, however, that debtor laws and vagrancy laws were needed in many cases to create a profitable postslavery labor system (see Crafton 1974; Williams 1944).

Why was the United States the only country in which the abolition of slavery resulted from a civil war? From the beginning, some of the opponents of slavery were motivated by moral concerns whereas others were simply looking at the interests of the White nation. Much of the effort to end the importing of slaves was motivated by the realization that if the trade continued, there would be an African American majority in many regions of the South and the whole South could become majority African American. Benjamin Franklin said with alarm that importing slaves had "blacken'd half America" (Jordon 1969:270). As White intellectuals and political leaders in the 18th and 19th century struggled with the problem of what to do with the slaves once they were freed, one fantasy was especially popular. Somehow, when the planter class was through with them, Blacks would be removed from the country. In effect, they tried to believe that African American people were what European's today call "guest workers." Essentially, there were three schemes to rid the country of African American people after slavery: send them back to Africa as in the case of the Liberian experiment, put them in the former Indian territories, or colonize them somewhere to the Caribbean or South America. When the Civil War began, there was no plan at all for what would become of the slaves if they were freed because there was no intention on the part of the Northern ruling class to free the slaves. Even after the Emancipation Proclamation, there was no plan for what would become of the former slaves. Lincoln continued to talk about and actually experiment with colonization. This confusion attests to the complexity of the contradictions comprising the productive system that had developed within the White and African American nations that had come to make up the United States.

Surprisingly, Marx and Lincoln, who communicated several times during the war, were in agreement about the root causes of the war. Karl Marx was always interested in the United States and he became a great student of the slave issue and the Civil War. He was employed to write analyses of the war for American and European newspapers. Marx maintained that the existence of slavery was a fundamental barrier to the liberation of the American working class. To Marx, the Civil War was the climatic resolution of the contradiction between two types of capitalism, the agrarian slave economy of the southern colonies and the developing agrarian, commercial, and industrial wage labor system of the North. The slave system only worked with large gangs of slaves working on wide expanses of fertile soil (Marx and Engels 1974). But because of the exhaustion of the soil, this system could only be sustained by territorial expansion. Where the soil cannot sustain slavery, the sale of slaves into expanding territories can. Thus, the planter class fought without quarter to expand slavery everywhere. Marx quoted a Senator Toombs at the Secessionist Congress as saying, "In 15 years more, without a great increase in slave territory, either the slaves must be permitted to flee from the Whites, or the Whites must flee from the slaves" (Marx and Engels 1974). Marx noted that expansion also served the planter class in that it could hold out hope to the ever-increasing poor Whites that they might become slave holders in the new territories (Marx and Engels 1974:69).

The drive for new slave territory took the form, politically, as the battle over seats in the U.S. Congress. After protracted conflicts, the Democratic party split into two parts, North and South, in 1860. This split made it possible for the new Republican party, which arose out of the armed conflict in Kansas over slavery, to elect Lincoln. Lincoln and the Republicans meant to stop the expansion of slavery while the southern Democrats argued that, constitutionally, all territories were potentially slave territories. Seeing that, politically, however, their fate was sealed, the planter class staked everything on one card, as Marx put it.

Marx noted that at its Secession Congress, the planter class invited all the states to join the Confederate states. If this had happened, he said, it would have resulted in the reorganization of the United States on the basis of slavery. Thus, Marx argued that the war was not really about secession. He noted that if just the disputed territories became part of the Confederacy, it would have held three fourths of what had been the United States. The planter class was in a war for the unlimited expansion of slavery and the control of the government of the United States. Marx (Marx and Engels 1974) wrote the following:

> The slave system would infect the whole Union. In the Northern states, where Negro slavery is in practice unworkable, the White working class would gradually be forced down to the level of helotry. (P. 81)

Here Marx was clearly saying that if White labor were to be placed in competition with slave labor, it would be a catastrophe for the White worker. He went on to say that the struggle was "nothing but the struggle between two social systems, the system of slavery and the system of free labor. . . . It can only be ended by the victory of one system or the other" (Marx and Engels 1974:81).

Although many in the English propertied classes wanted the government to support the Confederacy, much of the English working class did not. Lincoln's Emancipation Proclamation in 1863 produced a great enthusiasm among English workers for the Union cause. This may have been decisive in the decision of the English government to refrain from aiding the South (Du Bois 1935). Karl Marx drafted an address that was adopted by 6,000 people at a rally in Manchester. The address congratulated Lincoln and urged him to end slavery altogether. In his reply to Marx's address, Lincoln said that the Civil War was "the attempt to overthrow the government, which was built upon a foundation of human rights, and to substitute one which should rest exclusively on the basis of human slavery" (Du Bois 1935:91). Thus, Lincoln and Marx were in agreement as to what the war was really about.[3]

EMANCIPATION

In the middle of the Civil War, after suffering a number of military defeats and few victories, Lincoln declared the slaves of the rebel states emancipated and brought African American people into the Union army. Du Bois (1935) argued that after emancipation, slaves and free African American people greatly helped the North win the war. In addition to military action, slaves in the South engaged in a "general strike," spying, and widespread sabotage against the South.

The betrayal of the freed slaves after the war has a parallel in the bourgeois democratic revolutions in Europe that overthrew monarchies and the feudal order. The rising capitalist class aroused the peasant and lower classes with talk of freedom and liberty and enlisted them in the revolutions only to betray them after the fighting was done. In the French Revolution, it was the workers in the Paris Commune who were the power behind the victorious rising capitalist class. Here we see one ruling class inducing those oppressed by another, older, ruling class to join in the destruction of the obsolete social order. Similarly, in the American Civil War, Northern, antislavery politicians argued that the extension of slavery into new territories was a threat to the wage labor workers of the North. Conversely, slavery supporters like Henry Clay appealed to the Northern White workers to oppose abolition because the North would be flooded with African American competitors if slavery ended. In other words, when fundamental contradictions in a society erupt, the antagonists within the ruling class may well reach across each other to rouse the oppressed against their masters. There are real dangers, however, in doing this.

What Marx and other European revolutionaries came to realize from their study of the demise of feudalism and the triumph of capitalism was that it was precisely in the midst of the chaos created by the warring factions of the ruling class that a real revolution could be made. If the working class could wrest control of the struggle from a split ruling class, private property itself could be overthrown. In fact, all the communist revolutions that have succeeded have occurred in societies in the chaos that accompanies the transition from feudalism to capitalism. Marx may have thought that the

Civil War was a prelude to a new type of revolution in America. He moved the headquarters of the First International here in 1872 where it expired a few years later.[4] Emancipation of the slaves, after all, was one of the largest attacks on private capitalist property that had ever occurred.

As noted earlier, the Republicans had not intended to end slavery, only block its expansion, but in the midst of the war, Lincoln had no choice but to free them. The act of abolition had opened up dramatic possibilities for the expansion of equality and democracy in the country once the war was over. If planter's slaves could be taken without compensation, could not their land be taken also and given to those who had tilled it for centuries as slaves? If so, what about all tenant farmers throughout the country? And what about industrial workers who so often called themselves "wage slaves?" And if the freed slaves were to be given the vote, why not everybody, even women?

NOTES

1. Aptheker's (1969) work is a sobering corrective to the work of writers such as Elkins (1968) and Klein (1967). Where Aptheker unearths the actual, material resistance of slaves, Elkins and Klein focus on the written law and thus convey a false picture of a totally subjugated, unresisting slave. In Elkins work, this is summed up as the "Sambo." Although Elkins is outraged against the creation of the "Sambo," he inadvertently contributes to the ideological distortions of the slave condition and reflects the ideal planter view of the world. With this view, the contemporary African American person is bereft of the history of resistance to slavery.

2. As a general phenomenon, the modern capitalist state was often formed in such a way that diverse nations and sometimes hostile nations were incorporated within the same territory. In this context, the term *nation* was made to be synonymous with the state, hence the term *nation-state*. Where the state is dominated by a capitalist class of one particular nation, that nation becomes the oppressing nation and defines its interests as the interests of all nations. Thus, "the" nation is a conceptual way of negating the existence of other nations. Working people of the dominant nation derive real and also imagined benefits from their "kindred" ruling class and thus participate in the suppression of other, oppressed, nations but ultimately to their own determent. Whether it is race or religion that is used to characterize a people, they are in reality, nations, and as such they are of two basic types, oppressing nations and oppressed nations. Considering all of this, I use the term *race* in quotation marks to convey the racist meaning of the term. Race is a term that hides the reality of national oppression. I elaborate on this argument in Chapter 3, this volume.

3. Much earlier, in the Lincoln-Douglas debates, Lincoln had said, "a house divided against itself could not stand," and he said that the country would either be "all slave" or "all free."

4. Isaiah Berlin (1968) suggested that Marx moved the International to the United States to keep it out of the hands of Bakunin, a rival. That may have been a factor, but Marx clearly

anticipated that working-class struggle would greatly accelerate in the United States after the Civil War and, as it turned out, he was correct (see Chapter 3, this volume).

REFERENCES

Allen, Theodore W. 1994. *The Invention of the White Race.* Vol. 1. New York: Verso.

Aptheker, Herbert. 1969. *To Be Free: Studies in American Negro History.* New York: International Publishers.

Bennett, Lerone, Jr. 1982. *Before the Mayflower: A History of Black America.* New York: Penguin.

Berlin, Isaiah. 1968. *Karl Marx.* New York: Oxford University Press.

Breen, T. H. 1973. "A Changing Labor Force and Race Relations in Virginia 1660-1710." *Journal of Social History* 7:3-25.

Carr, Leslie G. 1981. "The Origins of the Communist Party's Black Nation Thesis." *Insurgent Sociologist* 10:35-49.

Costello, R. B., ed. 1995. *Webster's College Dictionary.* New York: Random House.

Crafton, Michael. 1974. *Sinews of Empire: As Short History of British Slavery.* New York: Anchor.

Du Bois, W. E. B. 1935. *Black Reconstruction.* New York: Russell and Russell.

Du Bois, W. E. B. 1967. *The Philadelphia Negro.* New York: Schocken.

Eastland, Terry and William Bennett. 1979. *Counting by Race.* New York: Basic Books.

Easton, Lloyd and Kurt Guddat. 1967. *Writings of the Young Marx on Philosophy and Society.* Garden City, NY: Doubleday.

Elkins, Stanley M. 1968. *Slavery.* Chicago: University of Chicago Press.

Foner, Eric. 1990. *A Short History of Reconstruction: 1863-1877.* New York: Harper and Row.

Frazier, Franklin. 1957. *Race and Culture Contracts in the Modern World.* Boston: Beacon.

Fresia, Jerry. 1988. *Toward an American Revolution.* Boston: South End Press.

Gutman, Herbert G. 1977. *The Black Family in Slavery and Freedom: 1750-1925.* New York: Vintage.

Jordon, Winthrop D. 1969. *White Over Black.* Baltimore: Penguin.

Klein, Herbert S. 1967. *Slavery in the Americas.* Chicago: University of Chicago Press.

Lively, Donald E. 1992. *The Constitution and Race.* New York: Praeger.

Marx, Karl and Frederick Engels. 1974. *The Civil War in the United States.* New York: International Publishers.

Morgan, Edmund S. 1975. *American Slavery, American Freedom: The Ordeal of Colonial Virginia.* New York: Norton.

Williams, Eric. 1944. *Capitalism and Slavery.* Chapel Hill: University of North Carolina Press.

Zinn, Howard. 1995. *A People's History of the United States: 1492-Present.* New York: Harper Perennial.

3

SHARECROPPING AND THE RISE OF EVOLUTIONARY "RACIST" IDEOLOGY

After the Civil War, various class forces contended in the South and between the South and the rest of the country to determine the status of the former slaves. Despite some early promising developments, the planter class returned to power in the South and the African American was reoppressed. During this time, at the peak of Western colonialism, evolutionary "racist" ideology became the dominant ideology on the subject of race throughout the capitalist world. This ideology was adopted in the United States with religious-like certainty especially in regard to African Americans.

ECONOMIC CONTRADICTIONS

In 1854, Lincoln confessed that he did not know what to do with the slaves if slavery was abolished. He wanted to send freed slaves to Liberia but felt that they would perish there. He said he personally could not treat them as equals in this country and was sure that that was the sentiment of most White people. In a speech in 1858, Lincoln opposed social and political equality, voting rights, and intermarriage and was of the opinion that if the two races had to live together, the White should be superior. In 1862, he favored colonization in South America. In his Annual Message to Congress in 1862, he recommended Liberia or Haiti as places for voluntary colonization. Lincoln had been petitioned by free African American people to help freed slaves leave the country. In this speech, he also addressed a major concern that he thought to be imaginary and malicious. He said the following (Jacobs and Landau 1971):

> It is insisted that their presence would injure and displace White labor and White laborers. Labor is like any other commodity in the market—increase the demand for it, and you increase the price of it. Reduce the supply of Black labor by colonizing the Black laborer out of the country, and by precisely so much you increase the demand for, and wage of, White labor.
>
> But it is dreaded that the freed people will swarm forth and cover the whole land? Are they not already in the land? Will liberation make them any more numerous? Equally distributed [sic] among the Whites of the whole country, and there would be but one colored to seven Whites. Could the one in any way greatly disturb the seven? (Pp. 159-162)

Thus, Lincoln acknowledged that the supply of labor affects wages but he argued that voluntary colonization and dispersal of freed slaves would minimize the effect. At his urging, Congress appropriated $600,000 to carry out an initial project. Lincoln had asked for $20,000,000. A contract was signed with a Bernard Kock who had leased an island near Haiti. Five hundred African Americans were taken to the island where 200 soon died. Lincoln brought back the survivors and the colonization bill was repealed by Congress (Bracey, Meier, and Rudwick 1970:197).

As we have seen, even in the colonial period White workers saw that slave labor was a threat to their wages and they fought to protect themselves. There is no doubt that many Northern White workers saw a serious threat in the liberation of African American slaves. Attacks occurred against African American workers even before the war began (Du Bois 1935). Prior to emancipation, attacks on African American people who had fled to the North from slavery occurred in Brooklyn, New York City, Chicago, Detroit, Boston, and St. Paul (Roediger 1992:172) and in Cincinnati, Toledo, and New Albany, Indiana (Steinberg 1989:177). The majority of White workers wanted African American people contained in the South. To that end, Pennsylvania, Ohio, and Illinois passed laws restricting African American migration (Steinberg 1989:181). Du Bois noted that there were 50 strikes between 1881 and 1900 in which White workers protested the employment of African American workers (Du Bois 1912).

The problem posed by the ex-slaves was interconnected with a number of other problems facing the Northern capitalist class once the Civil War was over. What should be done with the planter class in the South? How could the agrarian South be opened up to capitalist investment and development? How could southern cotton again be supplied to Northern and British mills so that prewar debts might be paid, and commerce resume with the South?

The planter class had dominated southern life and driven much of national politics from the beginning of the country. If this was to be truly changed after the war, the planter class should have been abolished as a class and the only way for that to have really happened would have been to deprive them of their land. In other words, the relations of production in the base of society had to be changed if the Civil War was going to result in the thorough transformation of the South, the condition of African American people, and the entire country. Despite the anger of important Northern politicians who knew exactly who had brought on the war, despite the genuine concern of some for the former slaves, despite the ambitions of capital to develop the South, despite federal experiments in land redistribution, military rule, dictated state constitutions, and protected voting rights, the final outcome was that the planter class retained its ownership of land and thus returned to power in the South. In the end, the planter class successfully used the most brutal terrorism including the Ku Klux Klan to destroy the fragile unity between the newly enfranchised African American and White working class in the South and thus preserved economic and political control. Scholars such as Du Bois (1935), C. Vann Woodward (1962), and John Hope Franklin (1994) are in agreement that the Northern ruling class failed to move against the private property of the planter class because of the fear that such a move would endanger capitalist property in general. A few "radicals" argued that the former slaves should be compensated for two and half centuries of forced labor by giving them the land that they had tilled. The fear was that this could set off not only an agrarian revolution of tenant farmers in the country but an industrial workers' revolution as well (Du Bois 1935).

Reconstruction could not carry out the task of land redistribution. In addition, Northern workers feared competition with the freed slaves and Northern capitalists wanted cotton production to resume. The outcome was that African American people came to be virtually reenslaved through a system of social organization, which came to be know as *sharecropping,* a system of debt peonage. The federally run Freedmen's Bureau actually set the stage for this soon after the end of the war by coercing freed slaves into signing labor contracts with plantation owners (Steinberg 1989:194). Thus, many African American people in the South were doomed to another 100 years of what was virtually forced labor under another name.

POLITICAL CONTRADICTIONS

Northern capitalism had prospered greatly during the Civil War from war contracts. After the war, as Foner (1990:10) put it, industrial capitalism advanced its interest, in the form of Republicanism "clothed" in the moral authority of having freed the slaves. One of the ironies of the Civil War was that poor Whites in the South received the vote along with freed slaves. This was done by the Republican Congress during Reconstruction to create a counter to the power of the planters. Reconstruction ended with the Compromise of 1876.[1] When federal troops were withdrawn from the South, the planter class was able to complete its return to power. The planter class supported the vote and certain civil rights for African Americans. They gained African American votes in exchange for protection from the crude and violent "racism" of the White working class (Woodward 1962). In other words, the class position of the planter class was expressed in their political orientation toward the African American. Because their property placed them above any threat from African Americans, they saw no reason why the African American should be denied the vote. The White working class, however, saw a grave threat from African American competition and acted on their fear with violence. Thus, we see how the contradiction of "race" can split a class and produce the political alignment of the most oppressed, African Americans, with the most elite, the planter class. The planter class courted Northern capital and supported economic policies that ran counter to agrarian interests. Severe economic recessions in the 1880s and 1890s created a climate of near revolt within the working class and among small farmers. It was in this context that the Populist movement swept across the South.

THE POPULIST MOVEMENT

C. Vann Woodward (1962) described the Populist Party as a genuinely equalitarian political movement that united White and African American in the South out of a common fight against "want and poverty." White Populists went over the heads of the paternalistic planters and, for a time, successfully appealed to African Americans on the basis of a common, class-based, self-interest. Tom Watson (Woodward 1962), a key leader of the movement, said to both races:

> You are made to hate each other because upon that hatred is rested the keystone of the arch of financial despotism that enslaves you both. You are deceived and blinded that you may not see how this race antagonism perpetuates a monetary system that beggars you both. (P. 45)

The response of the planter class was swift and deadly. Many White and African American elected officials were murdered across the South. A general reign of terror took the lives of thousands of others, mainly African Americans. The planter class mobilized poor White voters with an all-out racist campaign and they stole elections by fraudulently giving themselves "Black" votes that were not cast (Woodward 1962).

In Georgia in 1892 when a African American leader in the People's party was threatened with lynching, 2,000 armed White farmers responded to the call of the party's president to protect the man. The Georgia party adopted an antilynching plank in 1896 during the peak of lynching in that state. But in 1906, under the onslaught of what has been called a "second civil war" (Du Bois 1935), Tom Watson, the party's president, capitulated to the forces of racist terrorism. Watson delivered the Populist vote to the Democrat, Hoke Smith. Smith was the editor of the *Atlanta Journal.* During his run for governor, the paper ran a series of stories about atrocities supposedly committed by African Americans. Watson agreed to support Smith despite his announced intentions to disenfranchise African American voters because Smith said he would support Populist (class) reforms (Woodward 1962). Smith's campaign "first attacked corporations and then was suddenly twisted into scandalous traducing of the Negro race" (Du Bois 1935:701). Four days of race riots followed Hoke Smith's victory. Twenty-five African American men were murdered in the streets of Atlanta, hundreds suffered injuries, and more than 1,000 African American people fled from the city (Weinstein and Gatell 1970:128). This was just one of many "pogroms" that swept the South at this time.

The argument was made that peace would prevail in the South when White people stopped competing with each other for African American votes. After the turn of the century, disfranchisement of the African American swept across the South.

With it's one-party Democratic political system, the South became the impoverished, fear-ridden backwater of the nation. In retrospect, the extension of democracy during Reconstruction became not a solution to the problem of racism, but part of the problem. When Du Bois (1935) looked at what happened after the Compromise of 1876, he said of the South:

> After enslaving the Negro for two and one-half centuries, it turned on his emancipation to beat a beaten man, to trade in slaves, and to kill the defenseless; to break the spirit of the Black man and humiliate him into hopelessness; to establish a new dictatorship of property in the South through the color line. (P. 707)

These words and what they describe, haunt America to this day.

SEGREGATION

During Reconstruction the "races" were separated at church, in school, and in social life with little objection but attempts to segregate public facilities by law were thwarted. African Americans and Whites used most public facilities together without difficulty (Woodward 1962:15-26). "Jim Crow" public segregation was not universally instituted in the South until the turn of the century. Laws were written that required the physical separation of all African Americans from White people in public places such as theaters, restaurants, rest rooms, trains, street cars, and so forth. The purpose of these laws was to demonstrate the supremacy of the White nation over the African American nation. All Whites, regardless of their class, were made superior to all African American people regardless of their class.

UNIONS

The increasingly militant White working class in the North experienced great advances following the Civil War. Unionization and political organization helped produce labor legislation such as the 8-hour day for federal employees in 1868, public health measures, tax-supported public education, the establishment of local housing standards, the expansion of municipal services like gas and water, and so forth. But White labor had what Du Bois (1935) called "the blindspot" when it came to the plight of African American labor in the South. In other words, it was as if the African American worker did not exist. The labor movement of the North would have been much more powerful if it had been a united, nationwide movement but it was not. Northern labor was additionally split into well-paid skilled union labor and poorly paid African American migrant and immigrant labor (Du Bois 1935:584).

In the period after Reconstruction, northern labor unions supported the anti-big business Democratic party. African American people loyally supported the Republican party despite its abandonment of their cause and despite its identification as the party of big business (Du Bois 1935).

REAL INTERESTS, REAL DIVISIONS

To put it in general terms, the response of the workers of the dominant nation within a capitalist state to the threat of cheaper labor from another, oppressed, nation within the state, can take two basic directions: either against the capitalist class responsible for creating the competition or against the workers of the other nations. The first possibility goes in the direction of revolution and democracy, the second toward racism and fascism. Because the capitalist class normally has the armed might of the state at its disposal, it generally appears entirely too formidable to attack. It is much easier for racists to mobilize workers of the dominant nation to strike downward against workers of the subordinate nation than it is for revolutionaries to organize an attack upward against the ruling class.

The capitalist class had little incentive to stop attacks on workers of the oppressed nation. When White workers attack oppressed workers, they are actually preserving the oppressed status of that part of the labor force that must do the dirtiest and most dangerous work for minimal wages thus enhancing capitalist's profits. Time and again, police stood by and watched anti-African American pogroms happen or actually joined in. In addition, although workers at the very bottom would normally be expected to be the most revolutionary, in this case, they are isolated from the rest of the working class by racial differences, which has a dampening effect on class struggle in general.

Because of the interlocking of the race and the class contradictions, it is not uncommon for single uprisings to go one way then the other. In the case of Bacon's Rebellion (see Chapter 2, this volume), the attack was initially against Native Americans but then turned against the colonial ruling class. Conversely, a riot in 1835 in Baltimore started out as an attack on the homes of bank directors and ended up as an attack on African American people (Roediger 1992:109). The so-called "draft riots" by Irish mobs in New York city in 1863 sprung from anger over the fact that the rich were allowed to buy a draft exemption and avoid serving in the Union army. Although government offices and homes of the rich were attacked, the riot turned into a vicious and deadly attack on African American people and, in the process, a home for African American orphans was burned down.

THE POLITICAL DIVIDEND

The division of the working class into antagonistic groups begins in the quest for cheap labor. It is inherent in the competitive nature of capitalism. This division may produce a political dividend as well as an economic one. Once racial contradictions are created they can provide the "divide and conquer" solution to the classic puzzle of how the rich can maintain economic inequality and at the same time expand "democracy." At the time of Revolution, the founder, James Madison (Fresia 1988), put the problem this way:

> The landed interest, at present, is prevalent, but in process of time . . . when the number of landholders shall be comparatively small . . . will not the landed interest be overbalanced in future elections? . . . In England, at this day, if elections were open to all classes of people, the property of landed proprietors would be insecure. An agrarian law would take place. . . . Thus landholders ought to have a share in the government, to support these invaluable interests, and to balance and check the other. They ought to be so constituted as to protect the minority of the opulent against the majority. (P. 55)

Minority rights, meaning the rights of the rich minority to protect their property from the majority without property, were, in fact, established in such things as a Congress divided into two houses. Another device was the electoral college, which prevents the direct election of the president. This arrangement facilitated the collapse of Reconstruction in the Compromise of 1876. The initial solution to the problem of minority rule, of course, was to let the states make political participation contingent on owning property. Later, then, the division of labor by race becomes not just a source of wealth, but a means to protect wealth from class antagonisms while extending the vote. Extending the vote, of course, increases the legitimacy of government and of the whole social structure of inequality because it said to be the "will of the people."

Working-class White people have both real class interests and real race interests. The role of the political race demagogue is to articulate both interests gaining the votes of the White working class with the intention of diverting all class antagonism into racial antagonism. This diverting is what gains the financial support of the capitalist class. Although the behavior of the White worker appears "irrational" to the leftist intellectual[2] who sees the whole picture, it does not appear irrational to the White worker who sees the immediate advantage in maintaining his or her position above the workers of the oppressed race. Real race interests are what is at the heart of the racism of the White working class. "Prejudice" follows from these interests. If it is true that socialism cannot come about without multinational unity, the barrier to that unity is not just a matter of "attitudes" or "consciousness." It is socialism that tends to appear as "pie in the sky" against the real, material advantages that White workers have enjoyed. If the world existed as some Marxists described it, as a simple division between capitalists and workers, there is little doubt that workers would make revolutions. The colonial ruling class figured that out in the 17th century following Bacon's rebellion. They found that revolutionary impulses toward "leveling" could be stopped by splitting the labor force along racial lines and giving tangible privileges to the White worker.

"Reaction" is the way in which "managed revolutions" are brought under control. With the end of Reconstruction, racist reaction stabilized the new arrangements of property and labor and suppressed the forces of egalitarianism that had been released while fundamental contradictions in the society were being transformed into new contradictions. The new set of contradictions led to adoption of a new, especially virulent, racist ideology.

EVOLUTIONARY RACIST IDEOLOGY

Evolutionary racist ideology is based on the argument that different races of people exist in the world and they vary innately in such things as intelligence, morality, and their capacity for civilization. As noted in Chapter 2, intellectuals in the late 17th century such as Thomas Jefferson speculated that African people were somehow innately inferior. But it was not until the mid-17th century that the argument became the dominant ideology. Stephen Jay Gould (1981) has suggested that these "mistaken" ideas should be called "scientific racism" because they were advanced by so many 19th-century scientists. Evidently, Gould is not familiar with the concept of ideology. The ideas that he so skillfully debunked were clearly an ideology, not a mistake, and the scientists in question were precisely those intellectuals described by Marx as ideologists. I will use the term *evolutionary racism* instead of scientific racism because a later generation of social scientists also created a scientific racism, but without biological determinism.

It was the evolution of western societies that produced the ideology of human evolutionary racial superiority and inferiority. Although religion provided the primary racist ideology of early colonial capitalism, it was science that provided the primary racist ideology of industrial capitalism. By the mid-19th century the capitalist revolutions against feudalism in western Europe were more or less secure. Now instead of speaking of revolution, the capitalist class spoke of revolutions that went too far, against capitalist property instead of feudal property.

In this new age, competitive capitalism demanded the scientific improvement of the means of production so science was nurtured and elevated as never before. Scientific discoveries, in turn, dazzled the capitalist world. For many, science eclipsed religion as the way to understand the world. Thus, although the new racist ideology was quite metaphysical, it was always presented as "science."

Racist ideology grew out of a mix of reactionary and conservative thought. Reactionaries denounced capitalism and advocated a return to the status quo ante, to monarchy and the church, whereas conservatives argued for the status quo, capitalism without further change.

The reactionary, Count Arthur de Gobineau, was a French Catholic royalist, who wrote four volumes titled *Essay on the Inequality of Human Races,* which was first published in 1854. Gobineau's works were popular in the United States as a defense of slavery and in the next century they were of particular interest to the European Nazi movement. He clearly despised all notions of equality, democracy, and socialism (Gossett 1964).

Gobineau used the concept of race in a variety of ways. On one hand he saw three races in the world, White, Yellow, and Black, ranked in that order. But he also argued that nations were races, and even classes within nations were races. To illustrate this last point, Gobineau decried the impotence of the aristocracy and the rising power of the bourgeoisie in postrevolutionary France. "Money has killed everything," he wrote. The French Revolution had deposed the competent race, the race of princes who had descended from the ancient, blond Teutons or Aryans. The revolutionaries were of inferior lineages, whether bourgeois or from the lower classes.

As an aristocrat ruined by the French Revolution, Gobineau is an interesting transitional figure between feudal and capitalist thought. Feudal claims to property, power, and privilege were hereditary claims (backed up by "God" and divine right). The bourgeois revolutions destroyed the legitimacy of such justifications of feudal inequality. So, Gobineau sought to reinforce the hereditary claims of the monarchy and nobility with a new kind of hereditary entitlement. It was now racial superiority that justified the rule and property of a lineage. Those of a common lineage, "a race," have a right to have more than others because they are superior. Thus, a race became entitled in a modern way. In addition, the existence of a superior race is functionally indispensable to civilization. It was race that determined whether or not there could even be civilization. And, civilizations fell because of too much race mixing. The revolutions in Europe were uprisings of the inferior races and foretold the end of civilization everywhere. In addition to applying the notion of innate differences to race, nation, and class, Gobineau applied it to gender too. He explained the inequality of women in terms of their inferior mental abilities. They were not logical (Gossett 1964).

Gobineau himself, however, employed a type of circular reasoning that has been quite common among racists. He argued that inequality was not a socially created phenomenon but a racial one. Those with property and power have something special in their racial heritage that explains how they got what they have. How do we know that this special thing exists? Because they have property and power.

Many other European and American intellectuals and scientists published works that were similar in theme to Gobineau but more "scientific." Before the Civil War, the American scientist and physician, Samuel G. Morton, collected more than a thousand skulls from around the world to show that skull size and therefore brain size was related to race and it was brain size that determined cultural development. More than a century later, Stephen Jay Gould (1981:54-8) went to the trouble to show that Morton had manipulated his data so that his measurements would correspond to the desired ranking of races.

The international links between racist intellectuals are illustrated by the fact that Morton was influenced by the French anatomist, Cuvier. Cuvier, also influenced Robert Knox in England, who founded the Anthropological Society of London in 1863. Knox's society was modeled on the society founded by the noted racist, Paul Broca, in Paris. Knox is remembered for having said, "Race is everything" (Gossett 1964) and Broca for his conclusion that Negroes and women are like children in terms of mental development (Gould 1981). It should be noted that racist ideology was part of the rationale for the infamous Dred Scot decision in 1857. In that decision, Supreme Court Justice Tanney argued that fugitive slaves were property and had to be returned to their owners. Furthermore, slaves and their descendants were not citizens and had no rights because they were beings "of an inferior order" (Eastland and Bennett 1979:47). This is one of a number of instances that can be identified in which racist ideology became law.

Charles Darwin gave unprecedented credibility to the racist thesis. Darwin published his *Origins of the Species* in 1859. The prestige that his scientific accomplishments brought him imparted enormous influence to the racist views that he held about the human race. Darwin repeated many of the popular racist views of his day, particularly in *The Descent of Man* published in 1871. He accepted the work of those who had found meaningful differences between "the skulls of savage and civilized races" (Banton and Harwood 1975:36). He tacitly justified the English oppression of the Irish when he agreed that the Saxons were innately superior to the Celts. He saw natural selection at work in the genocide carried out by the British against the native people of Tasmania (Banton and Harwood 1975). He saw that Hottentots were intermediate between apes and humans and, in the *The Descent of Man,* the Negro or Australian was seen as being intermediate between the Caucasian and the gorilla (Gould 1981). Darwin (Haller 1963) also wrote the following:

> We civilized men . . . do our utmost to check the process of elimination; we build asylums for the imbecile, the maimed, and the sick; we institute poor laws; and our medical men exert their utmost skill to save the life of every one to the last moment. . . . Thus the weak member of civilized societies propagate their kind. No one who has attended to the breeding of domestic animals will doubt that this must be highly injurious to the race of man. (P. 4)

Here Darwin thought, in Lamarckinan fashion, that acquired traits such as poverty, injury, and illness could be passed on. More important, when he implied that interference with the process of "elimination" weakened the human race, he was paving the way for the eugenics movement, which would later promote the segregation and serialization of the "unfit."

Lombroso wrote on the evolutionary cause of criminal behavior and published his findings in 1897. The criminal, he argued, was the result of atavism, the criminal was a "throwback" to the primitive savage. The criminal could be identified by a variety of physical traits as well as such things as a fondness for tattoos. It followed, of course, that the savage was a criminal by nature. The notion of atavism is consistent with the notion of "reversion" or "mongrelization" that was popular among racists at that time. Reversion was what happened when the races were mixed. It was said that the offspring mainly had the traits of the more primitive of the two races that were mixed. Sometimes it was argued that the offspring had the worst traits of both races. At any rate, it was agreed that any race mixing with the Black race produced particularly deficient offspring (Gossett 1964).

AFRICAN AMERICANS AND WHITE LABOR

As previously noted, from the colonial period on, the ruling class of the American White nation entitled White workers to special privileges over African Americans. The notion that this entitlement was related to racial superiority was readily accepted by the White working class. But contrary to the traditional entitlements of White labor, White capital ruthlessly employed African Americans to combat increasing unionization and labor militancy around the turn of the century.

Booker T. Washington, the African American President of the Tuskegee Institute, made a famous speech in Atlanta in 1895. This speech is remembered as one of extreme accommodation to racial oppression. He said, "The wisest among my race understand that the agitation of questions of social equality is the extremest folly" (Zinn 1995:204). In that same speech, he urged employers to hire African American workers. He said that Negroes did not go on strike or engage in labor wars but were the "most patient, faithful, law-abiding, and unresentful people that the world has seen" (Zinn 1995:203).

African American workers, having been excluded from most unions, felt little solidarity with White strikers. Bonacich (1976) lists 25 instances in which African American workers were used as strikebreakers in 14 different industries between 1916 and 1934. She noted that between 30,000 and 40,000 African American "scabs" were brought in to help defeat the great steel strike of 1919 (Bonacich 1976:40). Striking workers, of course, are prone to be violent toward all scabs, regardless of race. Nevertheless, capital generally has the upper hand in these conflicts because it can use the courts and the power of the state to protect strikebreakers. The first big wave of African American migration to the North occurred during World War I when European immigration dropped sharply. After the war, in the summer of 1919, 26 "race riots" or pogroms occurred across the country as White workers tried to drive out African American competitors (Haywood 1978). Over 30 African American people were killed and hundreds were wounded in Chicago (Kerner 1968:219). In east St. Louis, hundreds were killed by mobs, militia, and police and 6,000 were driven from their homes (Jacobs and Landau 1971:175).

Confronted by the increasing power of an organized work force, capitalists suspended White national privileges and dealt with class conflict by employing African Americans. Thus, class conflict was turned into a conflict between the workers of two nations, White and African American. Political demagogues, then, could win office by appealing to White supremacist, racial sentiments—all the while taking capitalist money. Those who tried to unite African American and White workers against a common class enemy were called "Reds" or "foreigners" and, in some cases, this was not far from the truth.

IMMIGRATION AND THE RED SCARE

Capitalists used immigrants as well as African American workers to break strikes and destroy union organizing.

So, immigrants were also sometimes attacked or run out of town by irate workers when they were used as strikebreakers. In addition, it is generally agreed that, immigration keeps wages down. That is why capitalists favor it. But under some conditions, immigration may be a real threat to capital.

The first immigrant "scare" occurred in 1798 when the Federalists passed three Alien Acts restricting citizenship, giving the president the power to expel foreigners, and to have power over aliens in time of war. The fear was that immigrants from France might import some of the revolutionary ideas associated with the French Revolution.

A second and similar immigrant scare occurred in the early 20th century. About 14,000,000 immigrants had entered the country between 1900 and 1920 (Zinn 1995:373). This was a time of extraordinary labor militancy. Huge strikes, pitched battles with Pinkerton agents, police, and army units took place. Among the immigrants, a number of workers who came to this country were already socialists, communists, and anarchists. They combined with like-minded American citizens and ordinary workers to fight for better wages and working conditions. More immigrants came from Germany than any other European country during this period.[3]

During World War I, state governments, and the federal government as well, began using deportation of German aliens as a weapon against organized labor, arguing that strikers were disloyal to the war effort. In

1918, Congress passed the Sedition Act that provided a 20-year sentence for disloyal opinion or contempt for the flag or the constitution. Congress also passed a bill authorizing deportation for people belonging to any organization that advocated revolt or sabotage. The Justice Department found a way to strip naturalized Germans of their citizenship and deport them. The Justice Department also formed patriotic groups to spy on immigrants. These groups sometimes carried out vigilante attacks on their own. Deportation was specifically used against the International Workers of the World (IWW) because of its socialist militancy and its opposition to the war (Gossett 1964).

After the war, deportation became a major weapon in 1919 as fear that something such as the Russian Revolution of 1917 would sweep the country. Attorney General A. Mitchell Palmer, and the young J. Edgar Hoover, initially launched raids in 11 cities rounding up hundreds of suspected "Reds." Two hundred and fifty were deported to Russia. Two months later, 4,000 more were seized in 33 cities in 23 states and held for months without charges or being brought to trial until 556 were deported. The offices and presses of left-wing organizations were destroyed in these raids. Attorney General Palmer went to the prisons and described what he saw (Coben 1964):

> Out of the sly and crafty eyes of many of them leap cupidity, cruelty, insanity, and crime; from their lopsided faces, sloping brows, and misshapen features may be recognized the criminal type. (P. 198)

Palmer might well have been reading works of the prolific Lothrop Stoddard. Stoddard, who enjoyed Gobineau, was a Harvard doctoral graduate whose articles and books were quite popular in certain circles. In *The Revolt Against Civilization,* he wrote, "Now in this conflict the ultimate antagonists appear to be biology and Bolshevism: Bolshevism, the incarnation of the atavistic past; biology, the hope of a progressive future" (Stoddard 1920:237). In *The Rising Tide of Color Against White World Supremacy,* Stoddard (1922) wrote the following:

> Bolshevik agitators whisper in the ears of discontented colored men their gospel of hatred and revenge. Every nationalist aspiration, every political grievance, every social discrimination, is fuel for Bolshevism's hellish incitement to racial as well as to class war. (P. 22)

Stoddard said that the Bolsheviks had to be crushed with "iron heels."

What does it mean that people like Palmer and Stoddard found the Reds to be racial degenerates? Understanding this clarifies the methodology of the racists and it tells us what races really were to them. Where Marxists see social contradictions, the racist calls the oppressing side of the contradiction a superior race whereas the oppressed side is declared an inferior race. In this ideological formulation, contradictions are not denied by the racist, they are seen as the result of racial conflict and thus as the product of a natural law. In the case of the "Red Scare," racism was used as an ideological device to justify the unconstitutional and illegal breaking up of unions and political parties that confronted the capitalist class. J. Edgar Hoover, of course, went on to carry out many illegal actions against similar targets throughout his long career as director of the Federal Bureau of Investigation (Perkus 1975).

Stoddard acknowledged that employers gain by importing cheap labor. But, to him, the temptation to the employer was understandable. They are tempted to "put private interest above racial duty" where "white labor is scarce and dictatorial," said Stoddard (1922:274). He was particularly concerned about the threat of Chinese immigration. He said the "coolie" is the "ideal industrial machine, the perfect human ox. He will transform less food into more work, with less administrative friction than any other creature" (Stoddard 1922:276). Employers, after all, have to compete with each other once the employment of such "ideal" labor starts.

Stoddard (1922) explained that the White worker had to be protected from competition with certain immigrants because some races, such as the Chinese, could exist on practically nothing. He cited the sociologist Edward Ross, who said about Chinese and Irish competition that

> under bad conditions the yellow man can best the White man, because he can better endure spoiled food, poor clothing, foul air, noise, heat, dirt, discomfort, and microbes. Reilly can outdo Ah-San, but Ah-San can underlive Reilly. (P. 274-5)

President Harding endorsed Stoddard's books and Calvin Coolidge used racist arguments to advocate restricted immigration. Madison Grant, an admirer of Stoddard, wrote *The Passing of the Great Race* in 1916. He decried the entry of immigrants from eastern and southern Europe because of their inferior racial character (Higham 1981). Grant also wrote: "Negroes are never socialists and labor unionists and therefore not as dangerous as the immigrants" (Haller 1963:158).

Around this same time, the practice of "intelligence" testing was developed. A growing body of psychologists argued that mental ability was an inherited trait that could be assessed by responses to their tests. Wealthier people and their offspring scored higher on these tests while African American people, Jewish immigrants, immigrants from eastern and southern Europe, and so forth scored lower. Although these tests actually measured education and familiarity with American culture, they were accepted by many as scientific evidence of racial inferiority.

Albert Johnson, a key congressional leader for immigration restriction, was much impressed by Madison Grant's writings. Johnson consulted with Grant in the formulation of proposed legislation. It should also be noted that the American Federation of Labor, concerned about wage competition, supported restriction (Haller 1963:153). Congress found a way to restrict immigration "racially" without naming names. In 1924, it set a quota of 2 percent of those groups who were already in the country according to the 1890 census (Higham 1981:406). All "Orientals" were barred. The quota greatly reduced immigration, but it practically eliminated it from eastern and southern Europe. These were the poorest parts of Europe with the strongest socialist movements.

So, again we can trace the path of racist ideology into racist law. In this process, the socialist threat to capital was translated into a racial threat and produced what has been called racist repression. Organized labor was willing to cut off immigration to reduce wage competition while capital was willing to forego maximizing wage competition to reduce the prospects of revolution. The attack on immigration was a preemptive strike against the radical labor movement in the guise of race preservation.

EUGENICS

"Progress in the germ plasma" was the slogan of the racist movement. Stoddard was a "progressive" in the same way that Hitler was a "socialist." With the approval and support of the right-wing of the ruling class, they both proposed to rally the distressed working class against racial enemies thereby redirecting class antagonism into attacks on vulnerable minorities. In the racist view, social ills were not the product of social conditions. Nothing could be accomplished by changing institutions, but, because society was racially determined, progress could be made by controlling the "germ plasma," meaning the genetic inheritance of the race. This also meant that the defective could not really be improved or reformed but had to be eliminated. The eugenics movement proposed to breed a better human being. The superior types should be encouraged to have children whereas the lower orders should gradually disappear. As Darwin had suggested, the poor should not be helped with charity or welfare for that only enables them to reproduce (Haller 1963:4). This ideology later came to be known as Social Darwinism. In the United States, the eugenics movement was run by upper class "patricians" (Higham 1981). The movement succeeded in putting its doctrines into law at the state level. The idea was that the "unfit" could be "segregated" in institutions and when that proved to be too expensive, some were sterilized and released. Laughlin listed those as unfit who were: "feebleminded, insane, criminalistic, epileptic, inebriate, diseased, blind, deaf, deformed, and dependent (including orphans, . . . the homeless, tramps, and paupers)" (Haller 1963:133). Although the eugenics movement appeared in many countries, this country put eugenics into law 20 years before another followed suit. Several Scandinavian countries passed such laws in the 1920s. In America between 1907 and 1931, 30 states passed such laws. Three states rescinded them, and they were rarely used in some states. The Supreme Court held in 1927, however, that the state laws were constitutional. By 1958, about 70,000 people, primarily White people, had been sterilized (Haller 1963). The practice was finally ruled unconstitutional by federal courts in the 1970s. It was the European Nazi movement, of course, that put eugenics to work on a grand scale. In Germany, the Nazi government began its program of sterilization in 1933. It sterilized about 200,000 people and murdered untold millions.[4]

DISSENT

Banton and Harwood (1975) have noted that a small minority of scholars rejected evolutionary racism from the outset. Highly regarded intellectuals like Montesquieu, Alexis de Tocqueville, and John Stuart Mill attacked the whole idea. In the 20th century, the anthropologist, Franz Boas, wrote against the idea as did some African American scholars like Du Bois. As Marx observed, however, ideology is not destroyed by criticism, even if it is correct. Ideology ends when its material base ends.

Banton and Harwood (1975) also argued that because there never were any discrete, pure races of the type described by 19th-century racists, what actually separates one people from another are their social and cultural characteristics. They concluded that:

This means that anyone who writes about the social relations of groups should use not biological, but social labels, calling them nations, ethnic groups, classes, communities, and so on. (P. 61)

Today the "Irish problem" is not called a race problem although it once was. Why is the African American problem still called a race problem? As suggested in the previous chapter, *race* persists as the defining term because *nation,* the term that conveys the essence of what African Americans are, implies an impermissible status. The continuing use of the term race beyond the era of evolutionary racism is an ideological phenomenon.

Among the minority of dissenters to evolutionary racism in the 19th century were the leading Marxists theoreticians. They not only rejected evolutionary racism, but called for the liberation and equality of oppressed nations.

NOTES

1. In 1876, the Democratic candidate received more popular votes than the Republican. Hayes, the Republican, was made president because of a stalemate in the electoral college. In agreeing to let Hayes be president, the (Democratic) South was given the power to run its own affairs with the understanding that it would not reoppress African American people.

2. In a recent book, Theodore Allen (1994) argues that Irish American workers' fears of African American competition "had no basis in actual fact" (p. 194). He likens those who make this argument to Jesse Helm's and his attacks on affirmative action and to those who would "qualify" an anti-African American pogrom by making reference to labor competition. He argues that "the cause was not actual 'job competition'. Rather, the problem of job competition was cast in the mold of White supremacy as an integral part of the social control system" (p. 195). But Allen shortly contradicts himself in saying "There was indeed a real competition between Black bond-labor and Irish American . . . workers, that if understood would have provided a basis for a joint struggle against slavery" (p. 198). Allen clearly implies that historians who speak of "labor competition" and make "allusions to 'Negro strikebreakers'" are racists justifying racist actions (p. 192). W. E. B. Du Bois makes numerous references to "a real competition" between the White worker and both the slave and the free African American person. In fact, this competition is fundamental to Du Bois's brilliant analysis of the history of racism in the United States. The thesis in Allen's book is that racism is a social control device in its essence. Capitalists created it for the purpose of politically dividing and controlling labor. White workers have no race interests, only class interests but they are duped by racists into thinking otherwise. My argument, following Du Bois, is that White workers have two real interests, class and race. For the reasons discussed in the text, they generally end up acting on their race interests at the expense of their class interests. The White working class has always understood what the state can do to protect property and suppress workers. They also know that the state will not do the same to protect African American people. Allen says that Irish Americans "should" have supported abolition. I agree

as would Du Bois, Marx, and many others, but this does not explain why they did not. To attribute this to racism explains nothing. That the White worker's wages may sink along with the African American worker does not make the gap between the two any less real to the White worker.

3. In 1887, Friedrich Engels, Marx's intellectual partner, gave his appraisal of the situation in America. He noted that in only two years time intense class struggle had broken out in America. He referred to the great coal strike, the 8-hour day movement, the Knights of Labor organization, and the formation of the Socialist Labor Party. The Socialist Labor Party, he observed, was almost exclusively made up of German immigrants. He urged them to learn English and "fuse" with American workers as soon as possible to build a national political party (Feuer 1959:489).

4. The Fascist parties promised to redistribute, not capitalist wealth, but Jewish wealth to its followers. In such ways, socialist revolutionary energies were diverted away from the capitalist class and into reactionary racism.

REFERENCES

Allen, Theodore W. 1994. *The Invention of the White Race.* Vol. 1. New York: Verso.

Banton, Michael and Jonathan Harwood. 1975. *The Race Concept.* New York: Praeger.

Bonacich, Edna. 1976. "Advanced Capitalism and Black/White Race Relations in the United States: A Split Labor Market Interpretation." *American Sociological Review* 41:34-51.

Bracey, John H., August Meier, and Elliott Rudwick. 1970. *Black Nationalism in America.* New York: Bobbs-Merrill.

Coben, Stanley. 1964. "A study in Nativism: The American Red Scare of 1919-1920." *Political Science Quarterly* 79:52-75.

Du Bois, W. E. B. 1912. *The Negro Artisan.* Atlanta, GA: Atlanta University Press.

Du Bois, W. E. B. 1935. *Black Reconstruction.* New York: Russell and Russell.

Eastland, Terry and William Bennett. 1979. *Counting By Race.* New York: Basic Books.

Feuer, Lewis S. 1959. *Marx and Engels: Basic Writings on Politics and Philosophy.* New York: Anchor.

Foner, Eric. 1990. *A Short History of Reconstruction: 1863-1877.* New York: Harper and Row.

Franklin, John Hope. 1994. *Reconstruction After the Civil War.* Chicago: University of Chicago Press.

Fresia, Jerry. 1988. *Toward an American Revolution.* Boston: South End Press.

Gossett, Thomas F. 1964. *Race: The History of an Idea.* Dallas, TX: Southern Methodist University.

Gould, Stephen Jay. 1981. *The Mismeasure of Man.* New York: W. W. Norton.

Haller, Mark H. 1963. *Eugenics.* New Brunswick, NJ: Rutgers University Press.

Haywood, Harry. 1978. *Black Bolshevik.* Chicago: Liberator.

Higham, John. 1981. *Strangers in the Land.* Westport, CT: Greenwood.

Jacobs, Paul and Saul Landau. 1971. *To Serve the Devil.* Vol. 1. New York: Vintage.

Kerner, Otto. 1968. *U.S. Riot Commission Report.* New York: Bantam.

Perkus, Cathy. 1975. *Cointelpro.* New York: Monad.

Roediger, David R. 1992. *The Wages of Whiteness.* New York: Verso.

Steinberg, Stephen. 1989. *The Ethnic Myth.* Boston: Beacon.

Stoddard, Lothrop. 1920. *The Revolt Against Civilization.* New York: Charles Scribner's Sons.

Stoddard, Lothrop. 1922. *The Rising Tide of Color Against White World-Supremacy.* New York: Charles Scribner's Sons.

Weinstein, Allen and Frank Otto Gatell, eds. 1970. *The Segregation Era.* New York: Oxford University Press.

Woodward, C. Vann. 1962. *The Strange Career of Jim Crow.* New York: Oxford University Press.

Zinn, Howard. 1995. *A People's History of the United States: 1492-Present.* New York: Harper Perennial.

4

NATIONAL SELF-DETERMINATION AND THE CONSOCIATIONAL STATE

Switzerland became the first modern consociational nation-state in 1848. In the Swiss constitution, the people of Switzerland gave equal legal status to the German, French, and Italian languages. In 1938, the Romansch language, spoken by only 1 percent of the population, obtained recognition. Twenty-six *cantons,* or territories, correspond to linguistic-cultural groups. Children are schooled in their own languages in each *canton.* At the federal level, each *canton* is represented by two deputies in one house and by population in the other house. Minorities are overrepresented and have the power to block legislation. Great effort is made to obtain consensus in governmental matters. Political parties correspond to linguistic identification. Although some minor instances of tension between these internal nations have occurred, Switzerland has an extraordinary reputation as a peaceful and productive nation-state (Schmid 1981:1).

Lenin and his fellow revolutionaries eventually adopted the Swiss consociational system as the model for the USSR. Examples of other consociational societies today are Belgium, The Netherlands, Canada, and Yugoslavia before the fall of communism (Marger 1991:134-5). Some of the nation-states that broke away from the former Soviet Union are still consociational in their relations with their internal nations.

To their credit, the major 19th- and early 20th-century Marxist theoreticians seem completely immune to the doctrines of evolutionary racist ideology. Marx, Engels, and Lenin, for example, ignored it completely.

Apparently, they considered it so foolish that it was not worth their while to critique it or even mention it. There was no question in their minds that the development of human societies was a social phenomenon not a genetic one. Thus, they usually spoke of "nations" and not "races" when analyzing the relationships between peoples. On the few occasions that they did use the term *race,* they never implied that there were genetic differences between peoples.

Although many attributed the terrible poverty of Ireland in the 19th century to "racial" characteristics (see Allen 1994), Marx analyzed Ireland as an oppressed nation. In doing so, he found in Irish oppression, "the secret" that explained why the English working class was not very revolutionary. Later, Lenin drew on Marx's writings in concluding that the Soviet Union should employ the Swiss consociational model. Later yet, American Communists drew on Lenin, Marx, and others in concluding that the American race problem was, in fact, the problem of an oppressed nation.

IRELAND, AN OPPRESSED NATION

Toward the end of his career, Marx admitted in a series of letters that he had been wrong in his understanding of the interconnection between class and national relations in the case of England and Ireland. He wrote (Marx and Engels 1972) in 1869:

> For a long time I believed that it would be possible to overthrow the Irish regime by English working-class ascendancy. . . . Deeper study has now convinced me of the opposite. The English working class will never accomplish anything until it has got rid of Ireland. The lever must be applied in Ireland. That is why the Irish question is so important for the social movement in general. (P. 332)

Ireland was a nation that had been oppressed by the English ruling class for centuries. This oppression made an English working-class revolution impossible because, "the English people will remain tied to the leading-strings of the ruling classes, because it will have to join with them in a common front against Ireland (Marx and Engels 1972:330). The exploitation of Ireland is "the main *moral* strength" of the English ruling class (Marx and Engels 1972:335, emphasis added). Ireland

> steadily supplies its own surplus to the English labor market, and thus forces down wages and lowers the morale and material condition of the English working class. And most important of all! Every industrial and commercial center in England now possesses a working class *divided* into two *hostile* camps, English . . . and Irish. The ordinary English worker hates the Irish worker as a competitor who lowers his standard of life. (Pp. 336-7)

When Marx pointed out that the competition of Irish labor drove down English wages, he saw that national oppression was part of the base of English society. In other words, national relations are part of the relations of production just like class relations. On this material division, ideological and political elements were created in the superstructure, which not only sustained national oppression but simultaneously reinforced class oppression. Marx went on to describe how this worked:

> In relation to the Irish worker, he feels himself a member of the *ruling* nation and so turns himself into a tool of the aristocrats and capitalists of his country *against Ireland,* thus strengthening their domination *over himself.* He cherishes religious, social, and national prejudices against the Irish worker. His attitude toward him is much the same as that of the "poor Whites" to the "niggers" in the former slave states of the United States.
>
> This *antagonism* is artificially kept alive and intensified by the press, the pulpit, the comic papers, in short, by all the means at the disposal of the ruling classes. This antagonism is the *secret of the impotence of the English working class,* despite its organization. It is the secret by which the capitalist class maintains its power. And that class is fully aware of it. (Marx and Engels 1972:336-7)

Marx went on to say that the Communist International should openly side with the struggle for Irish independence.

Revolution would actually be easier in Ireland because "it is not a simple economic question but at the same time a national question (Marx and Engels 1972:331). In other words, whereas national oppression paralyzed class struggle in England, it facilitated class struggle in Ireland. The "lever" had to be applied in Ireland. But the question remained, how could English and Irish workers be united?

How Does One Transcend National Divisions?

A very important incident came up in the general council of the International regarding just how the Irish living and working in England should be admitted to the International. A Mr. Hales proposed that it be done in an *Irish-blind* manner, so to speak. Hales (Marx and Engels 1971) said that

> the fundamental principle of the association was to destroy all semblance of the nationalist doctrine, and remove all barriers that separated man from man. . . . The formation of the Irish branches in England could only keep alive that national antagonism that had unfortunately so long existed between the people of the two countries. (P. 301)

Hales wanted the Irish in England to be represented within the British Federal Council. He also said that the International had nothing to do with liberating Ireland. Engels successfully challenged Hales's position. Engels argued that given 700 years of conquest, Hales's proposal was "an insult to Irish working men" and the fact that the Irish spoke English did not deprive them of their rights as a nation. Engels (Marx and Engels 1972) went on to say the following:

> If members of a conquering nation called upon the nation they had conquered and continued to hold down to forget their specific nationality and position to "sink national differences" and so forth, that was not internationalism, it was nothing else but preaching submission to the yoke, and attempting to justify and perpetuate the dominion of the conqueror under the cloak of internationalism. It was sanctioning the belief, only too common among the English working men, that they were superior beings compared to the Irish, and as much an aristocracy as the mean Whites of the slave states considered themselves to be with regard to the Negroes. (P. 302-3)

Here Engels, obviously in agreement with Marx, articulated the principle that the right to nationhood of an oppressed nation had to be recognized. Anything less was an insult to the oppressed and an act that would exacerbate the feelings of national supremacy of the workers of the oppressing nation. Marx had found "the secret" of the ruling class for preventing revolution, national divisions within the working class. This kept the workers in "leading-strings" and gave the ruling class a type of "moral" (nationalist) appeal to unite the English of all classes against the Irish of all classes.

Hales's error is easy to make. After all, Marx made it for much of his life and, as we shall see, Lenin was seriously perplexed by the problem for a long time. To many people, it seems that it could only be racists or nationalists who are not "blind." According to Marx's theory of ideology, this is not a simple error in judgment. Hales's inversion appears correct, especially to members of the oppressing nation, because it arises from the material inversion of oppressor over oppressed, English over Irish, White nation over African American nation.

As Marx observed, nationalism or racism provides the ruling class with an opportunity to exercise moral (ideological) leadership. The ruling class righteously leads the other classes against the oppressed nation and protects them from it. Of course, it was the ruling class that incorporated or created the oppressed nation in the first place. If the ruling class succeeds in uniting all classes in the dominant nation against all classes in the oppressed nation, then total national oppression exists.

All-class unity is what generally happens in war between two countries also. The mystifying terms *race* and *racism* prevent us from seeing that wars of aggression and internal racial conflict are very similar phenomena, the conflict of nations. That is why "race traitors" (i.e., "White niggers") are treated much the same way by White nationalists as those who might protest a foreign war. Whereas racism in war is occasionally recognized (i.e., calling Vietnamese "Gooks"), White nationalism is not properly identified when African Americans are called "niggers" or people "lacking in values."

Mr. Hales, the English Marxist cited above, referred to "barriers that separated man from man." This is an example of the "left-wing," "progressive" supremacist cloaking his nationalism in a lofty, moralistic universalism. There are no English or Irish, only "men" said Hales. Thus, anything that even recognized the oppression that existed was itself a perpetuation of oppression. This is classic ideological inversion. It is precisely the same line of argument used today by the "color-blind" against affirmative action in the United States. They say that there is only one race, the human race—there are no White or African American people, just people. This is typically said with a glowing, religious-like expression of transcendent morality. This ideal universalism rises above the real world as a solution to real-world problems, while in that real world, people's eyes tell them that races exist and real problems exist between those races.

Marx and Engels would have none of what Hales was saying. But, it must be said that the difficulty of uniting those who are nationally divided cannot be underestimated. How do you convince people that giving up their material privileges will yield greater benefits? As Marx made clear himself, the Irish were a material threat[1] to the standard of living of the English working class in England and an enemy on the Irish battlefield as well. Support for the Irish worker tends to look like disloyalty to the English worker just as support for Irish independence looks like the actions of a traitor. If the International is an organization of disloyal traitors, how do you recruit workers into it?

Neither Marx nor Engels referred to African Americans as a nation, but, as seen here, they clearly saw close parallels between the Irish and African American situations. Lenin, however, after studying the matter, concluded that African Americans were an oppressed nation. Later, a number of people in the Third International studied and debated the question and eventually drew up a plan of action based on the general approach to the question of oppressed nations that had evolved in the International.

RUSSIA'S OPPRESSED NATIONS

Lenin had to come up with a way to hold Russia together when the revolution succeeded in overthrowing the feudal Czarist system. The Czarist empire consisted of perhaps 200 internal nations held together primarily by force. Not only were there many nations, but at the time of the revolution they varied enormously in development. Some had no written language and some in remote regions had not even been identified. Lenin was initially very confused about what course to take toward unification. The creation of capitalist states had required the destruction of feudal states and feudal federations. All "modernizers," capitalist and socialist, saw this as a progressive thing. Lenin, like Marx, saw the United States as the most advanced of the capitalist countries. He thought that the way in which the United States had assimilated European immigrants around the turn of century was a remarkable phenomenon. A unified people and a strong central government seemed to be the future of capitalist development and, according to Marxian theory, this paved the way for socialism and ultimately a world socialism that united the entire human population. The Russian revolution did not follow this process, of course. The revolution occurred in the transition from feudalism to capitalism so the break-up of feudal and prefeudal nations and assimilation had hardly begun.

In his initial writings, Lenin was adamantly opposed to anything that would preserve national divisions such as federation. He argued against the theory of Austro-cultural nationalism for this and other reasons. People like Otto Bauer and Karl Renner advocated a system in which everyone would have a national cultural identity regardless of where they lived within a country. The government would ensure equality of all cultural groups within a federation. There would be a "state of nations." In other words, the government could control prejudice and discrimination. Quotas for career opportunities would be employed even though this was admittedly inefficient (Armstrong 1977:94). This theory has obvious similarities with contemporary affirmative action programs in the United States.

Lenin not only opposed cultural nationalism because of its federalism, but because it was set within a reformist framework rather than a revolutionary one. It was developed as a set of proposals to reform the Hapsburg Empire in which nationalist groups were competing against socialist groups. Lenin saw these proposals as an idealist rather than a materialist way to attain socialism, tinkering with nationalism in the superstructure. As Lenin saw it, what was proposed was that a state, made up of cultural nations, could direct economic activity (capitalist) toward equality through such things as equal opportunity and equal pay (Lenin quoted in Lumer 1974). Lenin rejected the reformism but eventually, building on Marx's analysis of the Irish question, he concluded that a federated "state of nations" was the proper approach after a revolution but only if the nations were identified with territories. As a model for Russia, Lenin pointed to Switzerland (Lenin quoted in Lumer 1974).

The administrative efficiency of territories is obvious but it poses difficulties when nations are scattered. This was a big problem in the case of Jews who were scattered in various parts of Russia. Lenin insisted they were not a nation but later designated a territory for them. Apparently, this arrangement satisfied no one.

In addition to rejecting aspects of Austro-cultural nationalism, Lenin also argued against the "economists." Some among the revolutionaries argued that the existing nations in Russia would simply dissolve once socialism was established so there would be no national problem after the revolution. Lenin argued that this was an error, national differences would persist for a very long time (Lenin 1970).

Of course, Lenin also dismissed the bourgeois, capitalist political solution. In 1920, he wrote for the Second Congress of the reconstituted Communist International the following (Lenin quoted in Bhowal 1970):

> An abstract or formal posing of the problem of equality in general and national equality in particular is in the very nature of bourgeois democracy. Under the guise of the equality of the individual in general, bourgeois democracy proclaims the formal or legal equality of the property owner and the proletarian, the exploiter and the exploited, thereby grossly deceiving the oppressed

classes. On the plea that all men are absolutely equal, the bourgeoisie is transforming the idea of equality, which is itself a reflection of relations in commodity production, into a weapon in its struggle against the abolition of classes. The real meaning of the demand for equality consists in its being a demand for the abolition of classes. (P. 55)

Here Lenin was clearly building on Marx's critique of the capitalist-style freedom of the individual (see Chapter 1, this volume). He said that the capitalist way of handling the national question, the declaration of the freedom of all individuals, is an ideological statement that arises from the capitalist marketplace, from the system of commodity production. Capitalism handles national problems by pretending that oppressed nations do not exist just as it pretends that classes do not exist.

Lenin's position was that within Russia, there was "Great Russia," the oppressing nation, and perhaps 200 oppressed nations. The revolution by itself would not change that and the existence of these nations could not be ignored. Lenin's answer to the problem was that all the nations had the right of self-determination including the right to secede. His critics objected that if the oppressed nations of old Russia were given the right to secede, the bourgeois class of each nation would demand secession from a socialist state. Lenin believed that the ruling class could be isolated on this issue if the correct course was followed. He compared the question to that of the right of divorce, which the revolutionaries had also debated. Opponents of divorce had said it would weaken marriage. No, said Lenin, the right to divorce would strengthen marriage and, for the same reason, the right of nations to secede would strengthen the union of nations. The principle was that unity must be achieved voluntarily (Lenin in Bhowal 1970).

Lenin encountered much opposition to his arguments but just one month after the October Revolution in Russia in 1917, the Declaration of the Rights of the Nationalities of Russia was proclaimed. In it were four principles:

1. The equality and sovereignty of the nations of Russia;

2. The right of the nations of Russia to free self-determination including separation and the formation of independent states;

3. The removal of every and any national and national-religious privilege and restriction; and

4. The free development of the national minorities and ethnographic groups living within the confines of Russia (Lumer 1974:139).

This declaration was consciously constructed as the antithesis of the Declaration of the Rights of Man drafted during the French Revolution. After a century and a half, the critics of bourgeois constitutions had their day. In the place of a free "man" in the abstract, there were to be free and equal nations.

Within the Soviet Union, 177 nationalities received some type of recognition. There were 15 Union Republics, 16 autonomous republics, 9 autonomous regions, and 10 national areas or autonomous units (Davies 1978:91). One governing body was based on population alone, the other, the Council of Nationalities, was based on national territories (Haywood 1978:158). The self-determination policy "was to give each nationality administrative posts in proportion to its weight in the population of the territory (Davies 1978:92).

Lenin argued that the objective of self-determination was not to promote nationalism per se. Nationalism had two components, bourgeois and proletarian. The indiscriminate strengthening of nationalism could easily strengthen the power of the clergy, the rabbis, the landlords, and the bourgeoisie. These elements had always used national divisions to exploit working people. The ultimate goal was the "fusion" or "amalgamation" of the socialist, proletarian culture of the various nations. Federation, then, was a transitional form, nations would amalgamate far in the future (Lenin 1970). Thus, Lenin's approach was clearly dialectical. What he called "self-determination" was the resolution of the contradiction between assimilation and separatism. It is neither the assimilation of individuals nor the separatism of nations. Lenin felt that it was the principled way in which different nations could achieve unity and equality given socialism.

Rosa Luxemburg was a Polish Marxist theoretician who strongly criticized Lenin's slogan of self-determination for being entirely too vague. She preferred something like "freedom from oppression" instead. It should be noted that the slogan of "self-determination" was popular during this period of time in the capitalist world also. It was used uncritically in the capitalist world following World War I to divide up Eastern Europe and it has been widely used ever since. For example, following a period of strong Native American protest and activism in the 1960s, the United States Congress passed the Indian Self-Determination and Education Assistance Act in 1974. Few people would say that Native Americans really received the right of self-determination under this act except perhaps those who wrote the law.

Certainly, Luxemburg was correct. The term, *self-determination* is an extremely vague term and open to ideological abuse. For these reasons, in

1919, the Congress of the USSR removed the right of self-determination from the constitution but did not remove the right of secession. Davies noted, however, that the constitution of the USSR gave so much power to the central government that it had to be considered to have been "a highly centralized state" (Davies 1978).

Marxists argue that one of the laws of capitalism is the law of unequal development. Capital is invested according to the needs of capitalists to accumulate more capital and not according to the needs of people. Thus, cities are more developed than the rural regions, rich cities more than poor cities, rich races more than poor races, and so forth. Reformist redistribution of wealth can never be much more than tokenism against the law of uneven development. Revolutionary socialism, however, can direct the equivalent of capital to poor areas, Lenin argued. Socialist self-determination did not mean that each nation was free to go its own way or exploit other nations, it meant the strong helped the weak. Certainly in the early period, the USSR made a major effort to bring up the poorly developed internal nations (Slezkine 1994).

Assessing the strengths and weakness of the various phases of the Soviet approach to internal nations is beyond the scope of this book. Some, like Davies (1976), find significant merit in it whereas critics like Yuri Slezkine (1994) find it to have been an absurd and inherently contradictory set of policies.

In considering the consociational model, however, it is useful to contrast it with the way the United States "assimilated" Native American people. In the 1830s, the federal government initiated the Removal policy. Most Native American people east of the Mississippi River were forcibly removed to the west. In this process, the already "civilized" and Christianized Cherokees were taken on the Trail of Tears, a march on which about one fifth died. In 1871, Congress nullified the idea that Native American Indians were nations. Indians were declared incompetent wards of the government. In 1887, the Allotment Act was supposed to make Native Americans into farmers by parceling out national lands to individual Indians. In this way, two thirds of Native American land went into White ownership with much of the remaining land consisting of desert or semidesert. During this time, many Native American children were taken without the consent of their parents and put into boarding schools. Their hair was cut and they were dressed in clothing of the White nation. They were taught in English and any use of their own language was forbidden as was the practice of their own religion. Corporal punishment was administered to these children although it was virtually unknown among Native American people. Under the Termination policy of the 1950s, over 100 nations were unilaterally terminated. All special rights and treaties were abolished, national lands were to be parceled out to individuals but again most of the land ended up in White hands. In the 1970s, the policy of self-determination was adopted, which, at best, gave some limited control over education for the surviving Native American nations (Falkowski 1992; Washburn 1975). Native Americans are the poorest people in the United States today (Marger 1994).

What was done to Native Americans was tested and generally found to be constitutional just as the post-Civil War oppression of the African American was found to be constitutional. For our purposes, the consociational model gives us an antithetical perspective from which to see American race relations. From this perspective, we can see that it is not national differences that are bad. What is bad is the inequality of nations. In fact, saying that the differences between people must be eliminated so that they can become equal may not result in equality at all, but in the unilateral destruction of nations, the denial of the most elementary rights of national existence, the persistence of inequality, and the frustration and anger of all concerned.

MARXISTS AND THE AFRICAN AMERICAN NATION

Lenin arrived at the conclusion that African Americans were an oppressed nation as the result of his investigations that took place over a number of years. He referred to African Americans as a nation in 1913 (Lumer 1974:114), and in 1916 (Lenin 1970:118). In 1917, he wrote the following:

> In the United States only 11 percent of the population consists of Negroes (and also mulattos and Indians) who must be considered an oppressed nation, insofar as the equality, won in the Civil War of 1861-1865 and guaranteed by the constitution of the republic, has in reality been more and more restricted in many respects in the main center of the Negro population (in the South) with the transition from the progressive premonopolistic capitalism of 1860-1870 to the reactionary monopolistic capitalism (imperialism) of the latest epoch. (Lenin 1964: 276)

Then in 1920 Lenin (quoted in Bhowal 1970) wrote that communists should render direct aid to the revolutionary movements among the dependent and underprivileged nations (for example, Ireland, the American Negroes, and so forth) and in the colonies. (P. 58)

Between 1920 and 1928, the International sent resolutions or directives to the American party calling on it to improve its work among African Americans, but little was done. In 1928, there were only 50 African American members. The matter was being actively studied, however. A Japanese communist, Sen Katayama, lived in America for 26 years and attended Fisk University. He was considered an expert in the International on African American affairs. Several Russians, Mazaut, and Nasanov, also studied the situation in the early 1920s. A few African Americans began to study Marxism in the USSR where they compared their situation with revolutionaries from around the world. The first African American delegates to the International attended the Fourth Congress in 1922 where the first Negro Commission was set up. Finally, in 1928, after eight years of investigation and much debate and disagreement, a special subcommission was formed to draft a resolution to submit to the official Negro Commission of the Sixth Congress of the International. Harry Haywood, one of the African Americans on this commission, was the first in the group to grasp the meaning of Lenin's concept of self-determination. This happened in the context of trying to understand the powerful appeal of the Garvey Movement to African Americans. Garvey founded the United Negro Improvement Society (UNIA) in Jamaica in 1914. In America in the 1920s, the movement attracted tens of thousands of African Americans. Garvey advocated a return to Africa, promoted race pride, and Negro capitalism. He was a separatist who had some contact with openly White supremacist organizations. He was eventually jailed and deported for defrauding members of UNIA (Clarke 1974).

On the subcommission, predictably, the tendency was to dismiss all nationalism and argue for pure class struggle. Haywood, in contrast, argued that there was a progressive potential in movements like that of Garvey and that communists should not simply reject the nationalist movements that might arise among African Americans. In other words, in the subcommission, color-blind communists argued against those who had come to the position that African Americans were an oppressed nation with the right of self-determination. The latter position eventually became the majority position and the International adopted a resolution to that effect in 1928.[2] A series of three resolutions between 1928 and 1931 spelled out the details, which can be summarized as follows.

The majority of African Americans were agricultural laborers living under semifeudal, semislave conditions in the South. Here, this was an agrarian and national question and the main slogan of the party should be self-determination. This included the right of separation, which might or might not occur. Self-determination meant the unlimited right of the African American majority to govern the territory of the Black Belt[3] and to determine its relations with other nations, especially the United States. Land should be confiscated and redistributed to those who work on it. While capitalism existed, the party would support "national revolutionary" separatism among the Black masses, which called for a separate state, but not petty bourgeois separatism involving removal to an isolated place whether in Africa or America. If socialism came to power, the right to separate would be unconditional but the party would argue for the benefits of federation with a proletarian republic. Although it might be possible to win the right of self-determination under capitalism, this required a direct struggle with the bourgeois class and American imperialism and, to win, the support of the White proletariat was indispensable. The goal was not to achieve separation per se but to build an alliance between African American revolutionary nationalism and the White proletariat. Support for the African American national struggle in no way limited the fight, North and South, for complete and real equal rights for African American people. In the North, the main slogan for the African American national minority should be "equal rights." White workers must show their international solidarity by fighting in the forefront against lynching, segregation, and Jim Crow. All White chauvinism, or racism, must be eliminated in the party. Self-defense against the Ku Klux Klan should be carried out. Special attention must be given to Black women who suffer double oppression. The party must fight for the inclusion of African American workers in trade unions (which did not exclude, if necessary, their organization of separate unions). African American leadership must be built up in the party. Revolutionary African American workers should break down the mistrust that African American workers have of White workers. The party would not support bourgeois Black nationalism, which tried to develop a "pure" Black national culture and, which fought against progressive assimilationist tendencies of the African American proletariat. Black nationalist "moods" directed indiscriminately against all White people must be opposed (Carr 1981:46-7).

The adoption of this approach to the African American question was strongly resisted initially by many members of the American party, but over time the majority came to support it. In two years, Black membership went from 50 to 1,000 and by 1959 it was around 5,000 (Draper 1960:514).

One of the more remarkable products of this period was the Sharecropper's Union created by the Communist Party of the U.S.A. (CPUSA). In 1930, with the Depression underway, the party initially sent members to Birmingham, Alabama, to organize a steel workers union. Despite immediate violent attacks, this effort was expanded into a campaign to organize sharecroppers in the countryside. Haywood, who traveled to these areas, has related accounts of the murderous attacks on members of the sharecroppers union (SCU) by sheriffs and mobs (Haywood 1978). The sharecroppers, who were well armed, fought back and people were killed on both sides. Haywood said that the union had grown to about 10,000 members in five counties in Alabama by 1936. In addition, there were 2,500 members in four other states of the deep South. There were some poor Whites who joined the union. Haywood described it as an underground, armed movement. According to Haywood, what killed it was not the repression but a sudden switch in the "line" of the CPUSA. In 1935, Earl Browder, head of the party, began to take a more reformist political orientation. The SCU in Alabama was abruptly told to merge with a White farmers union. Haywood protested this decision. He pointed out the necessity of a Black union and the importance of adhering to the position adopted by the party in 1928, self-determination for the Black nation in the Black Belt South. Browder argued that Black and White needed to work together against a common class enemy and the SCU was a barrier to that unity (Haywood 1978:403). Browder's decision was part of a general move to the right by the CPUSA, so Haywood's protests were to no avail (Haywood 1978). The Sharecropper's Union quickly disappeared. The CPUSA terminated all work in the South by 1943, and in 1944 it officially repudiated the whole idea that African Americans were a nation entitled to the right of self-determination.

The leadership of the CPUSA had apparently expected that repression of the party could be avoided by becoming more moderate. But government repression of the CPUSA was unrelenting. The Smith Act of 1940 made "advocacy" a federal crime. Deeds were not required, alleged advocacy of revolution became a crime. Over 100 leaders of the CPUSA were prosecuted under this act in the 1950s (Church 1976:454). Many leaders spent up to five years in federal prison. In 1954, Congress passed the Communist Control Act (Church 1976), which provided that the CPUSA was not entitled to any of the rights, privileges, and immunities attendant upon legal bodies created under the jurisdiction of the laws of the United States. (P. 428)

In 1949 and 1950, conservative leaders of the CIO (Congress of Industrial Organizations) purged communists from 11 unions and expelled entire unions when the purges were resisted (Polenberg 1983:105-6).

COINTELPRO was a secret operation established in 1956 by the FBI to incapacitate Communists through the use of techniques that would "divide, confuse, weaken organizations" and sometimes cause "serious physical, emotional, or economic damage to its targets" (Church 1976:15-17). By 1960s, the FBI had files on 432,000 individuals considered to be "subversive" (Church 1976:451). This included members of civil rights and "Black nationalist" organizations, the New Left, and so forth.

Haywood was critical of the response of CPUSA to political repression. The response vacillated between disbanding altogether and becoming more and more liberal. Haywood preferred a more militant response. In his view, capitulation just invited more repression. The stage had been set for this, however, during World War II by the decision of the party to virtually eliminate any support for labor or the African American struggle and put everything into the war effort.

Having returned to an assimilationist, color-blind position on the African American question in the 1940s, the party's position was consistent with the reforms of the civil rights movement in the 1960s. Then, in the 1970s, the CPUSA stood on the sidelines and watched as an unprecedented, powerful, and sustained movement of revolutionary African American nationalism erupted from coast to coast.

STILL A NATION?

African Americans are no longer concentrated in the Black Belt South as agrarian sharecroppers. They are primarily urban and tend to be concentrated in certain areas but the areas are dispersed. Clearly, they are still oppressed but are they an oppressed nation? The transition from agrarian to urban concentrations does not mean that oppressing and oppressed nations are no longer nations, it means that the economic base of the oppression has changed.

Ireland has been transformed by urbanization, industrialization, immigration, migration, and division into North and South. Nevertheless, the

IRA in Northern Ireland has carried on urban warfare for 30 years. Because they still demand national independence and because it is no longer an agrarian question, what is the economic base of the struggle? The English-Protestant majority in the North clearly has dominance in the ownership of the means of production and in control of employment and the better jobs (Marger 1994:527-9). There is a "split-labor market." The English-Protestants view the Catholic-Irish as lazy, dirty, shiftless, oversexed, ignorant, quarrelsome, having big families, and inclined to cheat the welfare system (Marger 1994:526).[4] The split in the split-labor market still does today for the ruling class in England what it did 100 years ago when Marx discovered the secret of why the English workers were not revolutionary.

In short, the same processes of national oppression are still at work in both Ireland and the United States despite the changes that have occurred.

NOTES

1. Thus, national oppression is not the result of any set of ideas and overcoming national oppression is not a simple matter of overcoming prejudice, as the bourgeois social scientist explains it, or of false consciousness, as some Marxists explain it. These are idealist, not material, explanations.

2. A number of historians have argued that all of this was Stalin's idea and one that he imposed on an acquiescent American delegation even though it was a theory that was totally alien to American conditions. See Carr (1981) for a critique of these arguments.

3. The Black Belt was roughly the southern half of the cotton plantation states of the Confederacy in which the African Americans were the majority of the population.

4. The Canadian government undertook a massive study following armed conflict in 1990 with one of its "aboriginal" nations. The study, completed in 1996, declared that "Indian" nations had the right to self-determination and that the nations should have their own parliament. It was recommended that Canada negotiate on a nation-to-nation basis with the Indians. Massive spending was suggested to deal with the crime, poverty, alcoholism, drug addiction, family violence, and suicide that plagues the people of these nations. It was suggested, however, that it was unlikely that the recommendations would be implemented ("Study Urges Independence for Canada's Native People" 1996)

REFERENCES

Allen, Theodore W. 1994. *The Invention of the White Race.* Vol. 1. New York: Verso.
Armstrong, John A. 1977. "Federalism in the USSR: Ethnic and Territorial Aspects." *Journal of Federalism* 7:89-105.
Bhowal, P. C. 1970. *Selections from V. I. Lenin and J. V. Stalin on National and Colonial Questions.* Calcutta, India: Calcutta Book House.

Carr, Leslie G. 1981. "The Origins of the Communist Party's Black Nation Thesis." *Insurgent Sociologist* 10:35-49.

Church, Frank. 1976. *Book III, Final Report of Select Committee to Study Governmental Operations with Respect to Intelligence Activities.* Washington, DC: Government Printing Office.

Clarke, John Henrik. 1974. *Marcus Garvey and the Vision of Africa.* New York: Vintage.

Davies, Horace B. 1976. *The National Question: Selected Writings by Rosa Luxemburg.* New York: Monthly Review Press.

Davies, Horace B. 1978. *Toward A Marxist Theory of Nationalism.* New York: Monthly Review Press.

Draper, Theodore. 1960. *American Communism and Soviet Russia.* New York: Viking.

Falkowski, James E. 1992. *Indian Law/Race Law: A 500-Year History.* New York: Praeger.

Haywood, Harry. 1978. *Black Bolshevik: Autobiography of An Afro-American Communist.* Chicago: Lake View.

Lenin, V. I. 1964. *Collected Works, Volume 22.* Moscow, Russia: Progress Publishers.

Lenin, V. I. 1970. *National Liberation and Socialism and Imperialism: Selected Writings by V. I. Lenin.* New York: International Publishers.

Lumer, Hyman, ed. 1974. *Lenin on the Jewish Question.* New York: International Publishers.

Marger, Martin N. 1991. *Race and Ethnic Relations: American and Global Perspectives.* 2d ed. Belmont, CA: Wadsworth.

Marger, Martin N. 1994. *Race and Ethnic Relations: American and Global Perspectives.* 3d ed. Belmont, CA: Wadsworth.

Marx, Karl and Friedrich Engels. 1971. *Ireland and the Irish Question.* Moscow, Russia: Progress Publishers.

Marx, Karl and Friedrich Engels. 1972. *On Colonialism.* New York: International Publishers.

Polenberg, Richard. 1983. *One Nation Divisible.* New York: Penguin.

Schmid, Carol L. 1981. *Conflict and Consensus in Switzerland.* Berkeley: University of California Press.

Slezkine, Yuri. 1994. "The USSR as a Communal Apartment, or How a Socialist State Promoted Ethnic Particularism." *Slavic Review* 53:414-52.

"Study Urges Independence for Canada's Native People." 1996. *Boston Globe,* November 24.

Washburn, Wilcomb. 1975. *The Indian in America.* New York: Harper and Row.

5

PRELUDE TO "INTEGRATION"

The sharecropping relations of production in the South were brought to an end in the post-World War II period by technological innovation. As a result, African American migration to the cities accelerated. The ruling class examined the apartheid system of the old South and the developing "race" problem in relationship to its worldwide anticommunist strategy. Affirming that there was no African American nation, only cultureless and dependent individuals, it decided on a course of "color-blind" integration to resolve what remained of the old contradictions and contain the new ones.

THE END OF SHARECROPPING

Around the world the "agrarian problem" was the result of the contradiction between the private owners of agricultural land and those who labored on the land, the "tillers of the soil." It was a "problem" because from time to time desperately poor tillers or peasants had a tendency to resolve the contradiction by taking possession of the land. This demand for land took on revolutionary forms in the transition from feudalism to capitalism and in early capitalist development.

By the middle of the 20th century, the threat of agrarian revolution had disappeared in the most advanced capitalist countries because capitalist agriculture had progressively eliminated almost all of the agrarian workers. In 1860, 80 percent of the population of the United States lived in rural areas. By 1920, it was 50 percent rural and 50 percent urban. By 1990, the population was 25 percent rural and 75 percent urban (Macionis 1995:575). This last figure is misleading because many people living in rural areas do not engage in agriculture. By the 1960s, only 5 percent of the population lived on farms and only 3 percent of workers were engaged in agricultural production (Macionis 1995:575).

This remarkable migration to the cities was the result of technological changes, which were, in turn, the result of the imperative in capitalism to accumulate new capital. Competition drives capitalists to constantly transform the means of production to reduce labor costs. Science, harnessed to this task, produced a great variety of methods to increase agricultural output while reducing farm labor. So, in the end, the land did not go to the tillers, the land went to the agricultural capitalists and the tillers went to the factories. In the cities, the former farm workers were pitted against wave after wave of European immigrants and, increasingly, African American workers migrating from the South.

The displacement process developed more slowly in the South, especially with regard to the African Americans. In 1900, 90 percent of African Americans were still in the South and three fourths were in rural areas (Marger 1991:233). As noted in the previous chapter, during World War I, industrial production expanded rapidly while foreign immigration was greatly reduced by the war, so Northern capital recruited African American labor from the South to drive down wages. White labor in the North responded with a series of deadly pogroms. Nevertheless, this was the beginning of what would become a massive migration of African Americans out of the rural South. No demographic data exist on the size of the migration that took place during World War I (Taeuber and Taeuber 1969:12). Between 1920 and 1930, 700,000 left. Migration dropped to 350,000 during the Depression of 1929 to 1932. During World War II it increased to 1,200,000 and 1.4 million left in the 1960s.

African Americans made up 21 percent of the total population of the South in 1960 and 19 percent in 1969. Out-migration was offset to a degree by African American population increases. African Americans had a rate of population increase of 2.3 percent between 1960 and 1969 compared to a White increase of 1.2 percent (Simpson and Yinger 1972:313). Today, over half of the African American population still lives in the South.

Simpson and Yinger (1972) reviewed the impact of mechanization and chemical processes on African American farm labor. In 1958, 27 percent of the Mississippi Delta cotton crop was harvested by mechanical pickers. In just six years, 81 percent was harvested by machine. The smaller machines could pick an acre of cotton in 6 hours compared to 74 hours of hand labor (Simpson and Yinger 1972:317). One study showed that 90 percent of hand pickers in Arizona were eliminated by machines over a 10-year period. Herbicides and insecticides also greatly reduced the need for farm labor. In addition, foreign competition had an effect on cotton production. In 1955, the United States produced one half of the world's cotton, but by 1969 foreign competition had reduced that to one fifth. In sugar production, mechanical sugar cane cutters could cut 25 tons of cane in an hour compared to 2 tons cut in a day by one hand cutter. The total African American population on farms was cut in half between 1960 and 1972 (Simpson and Yinger 1985:171). In 1960, Washington, D.C., was the only city with a population greater than 100,000 in which African Americans made up more than half the population. By 1980, there were nine such cities (Simpson and Yinger 1985:172).

Thus, after three centuries, the southern planter class was through, more or less, with the African American farm laborer. In the past decades of this great exodus, the planters drove about 3,000,000 impoverished people into the cities of America. A major device in regional displacement derived from the right of each state to set the rules for eligibility for welfare and to set the level of welfare benefits. The southern states had the highest rate of rejection of applicants and extremely low welfare payments. In 1966, for example, welfare payments in Mississippi were $8 per person whereas they were $48 per person in New York (Simpson and Yinger 1972).

These migrants were ill-prepared for urban employment. The southern states traditionally spent between twice and 10 times as much on White education as African American education (Rose 1964:64). In 1959, 50 percent of all African Americans, North and South, had only an elementary school education or less compared to 19 percent of Whites. School days per year were much less for African American students, and African American teachers were paid much less than White teachers. In addition to very low levels of education, many of those displaced from the South displayed the effects of extreme poverty and inadequate health care. Infectious diseases such as syphilis and tuberculosis, for example, had not been adequately treated (Pettigrew 1964:83-7).

THE RULING CLASS PREPARES

As early as the mid-1930s, some American elites anticipated that they would eventually have to deal with the race problem that had been left in the hands of the southern planter class since the end of Reconstruction. In 1935, Newton D. Baker, Secretary of War in President Wilson's Cabinet, proposed that the Carnegie Corporation, of which he was a trustee, sponsor a comprehensive study of "the Negro in the United States." Baker was the son of a Confederate officer who became a prominent business and civic leader in Cleveland. As mayor of the city, he had become aware of some of the problems developing with the northward migration of African Americans (Southern 1987:3).

The Carnegie Corporation was the creation of Andrew Carnegie, one of the greatest "robber barons" in American history.[1] Carnegie was a great admirer of Booker T. Washington, the African American president of Tuskegee Institute. As previously noted, Washington was most famous for his Atlanta "accommodation" speech in 1895. In this speech, Washington explained to a cheering White audience that African American people had to improve themselves rather than agitate for equality. For about 20 years, Booker T. Washington was the person who spoke for all African Americans as a virtual "monarch," according to Bennett (1982:327). Washington, who had a white father, lived well and moved in high circles when in the North. Andrew Carnegie gave the Tuskegee Institute $600,000 in U.S. Steel bonds with the provision that Washington "be free from pecuniary cares that he may devote himself wholly to his great Mission" (cited in Bennett 1982:329). Washington's public statements never offended the White South. For example, he blamed a lynching on the lack of education of the person lynched and, on another occasion, said that lynching was not conducive to producing a reliable labor force (Bennett 1982:328). For a number of years after Carnegie's death in 1919, his corporation provided a "racial" fund that went entirely to African American educational institutions in the South. That was changed in 1935 when Baker persuaded the corporation to fund the study that would be known as *The American Dilemma.*

Gunnar Myrdal, a Swedish sociologist, was selected to head the study in 1938. Myrdal and his wife had spent a year in America as Rockefeller Fellows in 1929 to 1930 and Myrdal had given honorary lectures at Harvard University in 1937. Myrdal's initial rejection of the job offer was overcome when he was visited in Sweden by Beardsley Ruml of the Rockefeller Foundation. Myrdal was an anticommunist, Social Democrat (or left, liberal) active in Swedish politics (Southern 1987:13). He was a banker and an economic adviser to the Swedish government (Ellison 1973:91).

A large number of American sociologists and other social scientists were either employed or solicited to contribute to the study. Many African

American scholars questioned why an African American was not selected to head the study. A number did participate in the study, but because they so often failed to complete their work or complete it on time, some White scholars wondered if "passive resistance" was not occurring (Southern 1987:24). *An American Dilemma* was published in 1944 and the condensed version, *The Negro in America,* edited by Arnold Rose, was first published in 1948.

While in America, Myrdal had close contact with Walter White, Roy Wilkins, and Thurgood Marshall, major officers in the NAACP. Marshal was chief legal counsel for the NAACP and later became a member of the Supreme Court that ruled on critical civil rights cases. Myrdal, was "fast friends" with Supreme Court Justice Felix Frankfurter, and he had long discussions about the race problem with Frankfurter while working on the study (Southern 1987:129).

MYRDAL'S DILEMMAS

The book was essentially an argument for the integration of African Americans into White society. The main theory in the book was that this would happen because of the tension in the minds of White people over the discrepancy between the "American Creed" and the treatment of African Americans. That is, White Americans, who believed in the "essential dignity of the individual, of the basic equality of all men and of certain inalienable rights to freedom, justice, and fair opportunity" suffered from a "guilty conscience" because of the treatment of African Americans (Rose 1964:2, 319). In addition to this, it was argued that it would be extremely wasteful to the economy if 10 percent of the population (14,000,000 African Americans) were left in "the dependent category." It was also argued that the failure to integrate could lead to Nazi-like developments (Rose 1964:318-9).

But there was one final, critical, argument for integration. Integration was something that had to be done to thwart communism. In the last pages of Rose's (1964) book he states the following:

> America is now . . . a world power. She shares this position with Russia, and she is a competitor with Russia for world leadership. . . . The American Creed must, however, be lived up to if other nations are to believe what we say, and lived up to in regard to the Negroes as well as other groups. . . . Hatred of "White" people is intense in Asia and Africa, not only because the Whites

have set themselves up as racially superior but also because the Whites are seen as conquerors and as tyrants. *Hatred against Whites is identified with the struggle for national freedom . . . they have resented deeply our treatment of the Negroes and our theories of the racial inferiority of darker peoples.*

Until recently, what the colored peoples thought of us did not make much difference. Now it has become of crucial importance to us. Whatever Russia's faults may be, she has no color prejudice. *Again and again she has demonstrated that she does not regard colored people as inferior, that she respects their culture.* Laws against discrimination or the manifestation of prejudice are strictly enforced. To the colored peoples of the world, suffering under the double yoke of prejudice and colonial exploitation from White people, this attitude of Russia's has strong appeal. It is doubtful, however, if it is as appealing as the promise of real democracy American can hold out—provided we can hold out also *the promise of equality to the individual regardless of color.* (Pp. 319-20, emphasis added)

So, what "colored people" of the world thought of the United States did not matter before, but now it did matter very much because of Russia and the communist threat. The Soviet Union rejected the ideology of evolutionary racism, respected the culture of nations, and strictly enforced laws against prejudice and discrimination.

Myrdal (Rose 1964), who feared competition with the Russians because of their respect for culture, said this about American "Negro" culture:

For the most part, he (the African American) is not proud of those things in which he differs from the White American. Moreover, in practically all its differences, American Negro culture is not something independent of general American culture. *It is a distorted development, or an unhealthy condition of American culture.* The instability of the Negro family, the inadequacy of educational facilities for Negroes, the emotionalism in the Negro church, the insufficiency and unwholesomeness of Negro recreational activity, the excess of Negro sociable organizations, . . . crime rate . . . superstition . . . personality difficulties . . . are mainly forms of social ill-health created by caste pressures. . . . This can be said positively: It is to the advantage of American Negroes as individuals and as a group to become assimilated into American culture, to acquire the traits held in esteem by the dominant White Americans. (P. 294)

Ralph Ellison (1973), the noted African American author, wrote a stinging critique of this in 1944 but it was not printed until 1964. He said the following:

But can a people (its faith in an idealized American Creed notwithstanding) live and develop for over 300 years simply by *reacting?* Are American Negroes simply the creation of White men, or have they at least helped to create themselves out of what they found around them? Men have made a way of life in caves and upon cliffs, why cannot Negroes have made a life upon the horns of the White man's dilemma? (P. 94)

Ellison then pointed out that Myrdal equated "American" culture with White culture excluding all of African American culture. He noted that White culture included lynching, among other things, and wondered why the African Americans should exchange their "pathological culture" for another pathological culture. He suggested that it would take a "deeper science" than Myrdal's and that of contemporary "Negro scholars" to analyze the masses of African American people. He attributed the inadequacy of both to "clinging to the concept of 'race' " (Ellison 1973:94-5).

Myrdal was familiar with the Communist Party of the U.S.A.'s (CPUSA) proposal of self-determination for the oppressed African American nation and found it "fanciful" (Rose 1964:244). The passages cited earlier make it clear why he thought that the notion of an African American nation was nonsense—Negro culture was merely a "distorted" and "unhealthy" version of "the dominant White" American culture. Myrdal's views on African American "culture" are a perfect articulation of the White nationalism that is inherent in the classic liberal view. Myrdal noted with alarm the respect that the Russians had for the culture of oppressed nations. Yet knowing this and fearing this, Myrdal and his fellow-American social scientists looked at African Americans and saw no nation but only a race with a pathological reflection of the culture of the White nation.

C. Vann Woodward (1962) noted that in 1952 the United States Attorney General filed a brief in support of a school desegregation case that said the following:

It is in the context of the present world struggle between freedom and tyranny that the problem of racial discrimination must be viewed. . . . Racial discrimination furnishes grist for the Communist propaganda mills. (P. 120)

Woodward noted that within hours after the Supreme Court's school desegregation decision in 1954, the Voice of America broadcast the news to foreign countries in 35 languages.

He went on to say the following:

There was concern in high office not only for the struggle over allegiance of colored peoples in foreign lands but also for the allegiance of our own colored people at home. This was especially true with regard to the Negro intellectuals and the Negro labor leaders. Communist propaganda made a strong, powerfully organized, and concerted—if somewhat blundering—drive to alienate the Negro from his faith in American institutions. . . . The effect this campaign had may be detected in the Negro periodicals, literature, and pronouncements of the 1930s and 1940s, as well as among Negro leaders in cultural, intellectual, and labor fields. (Woodward 1962: 122)

Similarly, Myrdal (Rose 1964) said the following:

They [Communists] are the only American political group that has in practice offered Negroes full social equality, and this is highly valued not only among Negro intellectuals but much deeper down in the Negro community, particularly in the North. (P. 166)

Thus, there were really two "American dilemmas" in Myrdal's book and he cleverly connected them. The first was in the realm of ideas, the second was material. The idealist dilemma was in White minds and consisted of the American Creed versus American prejudice and discrimination. The materialist "dilemma" was the contradiction between the continuing oppression of the African American nation and the threat of communism, foreign and domestic. Myrdal's book was a great plea for the ruling class of America to prepare itself and the American people for a worldwide crusade against the Russians. The battle would be between the American Creed and Communism. One cannot help but wonder what would have happened to the new urban African Americans, or for that matter, the whole colonized world, in the absence of the communist threat.

Although Myrdal's study contains massive amounts of data on many subjects, there was nothing in the research to suggest that White Americans held within their minds a dilemma over race relations and the American Creed. The study did not even show that Americans held an American Creed. This was all an impassioned construction on the part of Myrdal. In fact, a series of studies that were conducted in the 1960s and 1970s found no support for Myrdal's dilemma. White people, who held various racist ideas, had a variety of ways of handling possible conflicts with presumably contrary ideals (see for example, Westie 1965; Caditz 1976; Wellman 1977). Nevertheless, Myrdal's dilemma became part of the ideological framework for the transformation of African American repression.

A great force was said to exist in the minds of White people that would change history. Material society would be transformed by the necessity of White people to resolve this mental contradiction. Thus, Myrdal's thesis was a classic case of ideological inversion. He argued that particular elements of the superstructure, thoughts in contradiction, would change the material base of society. He would have been hard put, of course, to explain why this mental force, which had been latent for 300 years, had suddenly become a decisive force by the mid-20th century.

Myrdal (1962) literally posed the problem in terms of "sin" and a "moral struggle" that had the potential for "redemption." He wrote on the last pages of his book:

> If America in actual practice could show the world a progressive trend by which the Negro became finally integrated into modern democracy, all mankind would be given faith again—it would have reason to believe that peace, progress, and order are feasible. And America would have a spiritual power . . . the trust and support of all good people on earth. *America is free to choose whether the Negro shall remain her liability or become her opportunity.* (P. 1022, emphasis added)

David Southern (1987) has suggested that Americans were set up for a dreadful disillusionment by Myrdal's moralizing. He said the following:

> In retrospect, one wonders why anyone ever viewed the race problem as an opportunity to precipitate utopia, especially when one realizes that the liberal solutions to the race problem, not to mention the radical ones, were so improbable. (P. 256)

But Myrdal gave the Carnegie Corporation the "social science" that it desired, a study that emphasized moral arguments rather than a materialist analysis of American race relations.

In the study, the way to transform American race relations was quite explicit. There was to be "equality of the individual regardless of color." This is the same language used in the amendments and laws passed during the Reconstruction period. Individuals regardless of their color should have equality. Individuals were to be given freedom *from* their race, not freedom *in* their race. This is the anti-nation, color-blind, integrationist approach. Nothing else could have come out of Myrdal's analysis because the culture of the "Negro race" was nothing but a "pathological" distortion of "American" culture.

The mind of the White person would finally be at rest once Negroes became individuals just like all other American individuals. Margaret Halsey wrote a book called *Color-Blind: A White Woman Looks at the Negro* in 1946. She argued that African American men had very little interest in White women contrary to prevailing "myths." She cited Myrdal, who had made the same argument. Margaret Mead (1946) reviewed the book favorably and found that it offered useful ways "to expedite the absorption of our Negro American citizens into full membership in our democracy (p. 14, emphasis added).

Thus, at the microlevel of interaction, where the problem was race, the solution was "absorption" or integration and the method was "color blindness." Just like European immigrants, the Negro would disappear into America. From the colonial period through the Civil War, the ruling class had promised White America that the African American would be removed through colonization when slavery was over. Instead, the African American nation was contained where it was, in the rural South. Now that that containment was broken, the plan was that the African American would disappear through color blindness.

The Race Problem Was a Caste Problem

Myrdal observed that the Negro problem was not a class problem because both Negro and White had classes within them. (It is not a class problem in this literal sense. Rather, it is a problem of economic inequality between nations compounded by class.) He rejected race because it inevitably implied genetic differences. "Minority group" was also rejected because it did not distinguish between White immigrants and Negroes. Although this much is well reasoned, Myrdal unfortunately declared that Negroes were a "caste."

The essence of caste was the inability to pass from one "status" to another (Myrdal 1962:668). Caste was defined in terms of its difference with class. Myrdal wrote the following:

> The boundary between Negro and white is not simply a class line that can be successfully crossed by education, integration into the national culture, and individual economic advancement. The boundary is fixed. . . . It is directed against the whole group. (P. 58)

And Rose (1964) wrote the following:

> Southern White opinion asks for a general order according to which *all* Negroes are placed under *all* White people and are excluded not only from the White man's society but also from the ordinary symbols of respect. (P. 26)

In the previous chapter, it was noted that national oppression is complete when a ruling class has succeeded in uniting all classes of the dominant nation against all classes of the oppressed nation. Thus, what Myrdal and Rose chose to call a "caste system" was really total national oppression. They could not have possibly used this term because they were certain that African Americans had no culture of their own. Myrdal does not offer a theory associated with the term caste. Rather, he offers a description of caste barriers such as prohibitions against intermarriage and intimate social interaction.

Even today, contemporary uses of the term caste do not offer much more than description. Marger (1991), for example, noted that a lower caste is a "pariah" group. This group must practice endogamy (marriage with one's own group), and is forbidden to have intimate interaction with the dominant group. Marger said in passing, "Subordinate castes are usually exploited occupationally" (p. 61). Marger also noted that, although racial differences are often associated with caste, that is not always the case. In Japan, for example, the Burakumin caste is not racially different from the rest of the population even though it has been historically defined as something less than human. Marger also pointed out the case of Jews who were forced by the Nazi to wear yellow stars of David for purposes of identification (Marger 1991:61). It might be noted that the Irish and English practice a high degree of endogamy in Northern Ireland but that is not called a caste situation. In short, it appears that what caste amounts to is a description of a set of practices that may occur within certain types of extreme national oppression.

The Rank Order of Discriminations

Myrdal asked many White and African American respondents to rank the importance to them of various forms of discrimination. He developed from this what he called a "rank order of discriminations." Whites ranked the importance of their practices in the following order:

1. Intermarriage and sex
2. Deferential etiquette

3. Segregation in schools, churches, public facilities

4. Political disfranchisement

5. Discrimination in courts of law, by police, and other public servants

6. Discrimination in securing land, credit, jobs, welfare

Myrdal said that this was the "White man's theory of color caste." In other words, White people explained to Myrdal why segregation existed and why it was so vitally important to them.

Myrdal (1962) believed that the White ranking was an inversion of a real or concealed rank order. He stated the following:

> Much material has, as we shall find, been brought together indicating that, among other things, *competitive economic interests,* which do not figure at all in the popular *rationalizations* referred to, play a decisive role. The announced concern about racial purity is, when this economic motive is taken into account, no longer awarded the exclusive role as the basic cause in the psychology of the race problem. (P. 59)

Myrdal knew that economic interests were really at the top of the list, not sex. But he dealt with this inversion by reducing it to a psychological phenomenon instead of treating it as an ideological one. Rationalization is what individuals do. The individuals he talked to could not have all come up with the same rationalizations. They expressed an ideological inversion of their institutions of segregation. As we have seen, in the mid-19th century, evolutionary racist ideology created an elaborate explanation for racial oppression. One of the justifications for national oppression put forward was the assertion that intermarriage between races would bring on the biological destruction of the superior race. What Myrdal documented in asking for a ranking of discriminations was that, among White people, this particular justification was passionately held above material interests. That is precisely the way ideology operates. It hides the world of material contradictions.

Rationalization did not explain why fears of miscegenation were at the top of the list. So, Myrdal further psychologized the matter by arguing that White people had intense and irrational sexual thoughts in their subconscious minds that were associated with their fear of amalgamation or miscegenation. He argued that these fears were the main element in the entire caste problem. Myrdal (1962) wrote as follows:

> This attitude of refusing to consider amalgamation—felt and expressed in the entire country—constitutes the center in the complex of attitudes which can be described as the "common denominator" in the problem. (P. 58)

Scholars who have described caste relations have always made prohibitions against intermarriage one of the defining elements. Myrdal made them the essence of the American caste system. But this seems to contradict what he had said earlier. It is not clear, but, perhaps, what Myrdal was saying was that although economic factors were the original heart of the matter, because of intense and irrational sexual fears, amalgamation had been transformed into the center of the caste problem for White people.

At any rate, Myrdal's psychological analysis of what was an ideological phenomenon did not clear up the mystery of the inverted White rankings, it made it even more of a mystery. In so doing, the "fear of amalgamation" was not relegated to the bottom of the White rankings, but was made the center of the caste phenomenon by Myrdal. Thus, a mysterious and irrational force was said to drive caste relations. In truth, the problem was not a caste problem, it was a national problem and amalgamation was not the center of the problem, it was a secondary part of it.

As suggested earlier in this book, intermarriage is an obvious threat to national domination. That was recognized as early as the colonial period in America. Intermarriage tangles families across national lines and makes such things as job discrimination, disenfranchisement, and segregation more difficult and it could allow property to be inherited across national boundaries. Nevertheless, what we can see today is that national oppression can be sustained without antimiscegenation laws.

What is fascinating about Myrdal's study of the "rank order of discriminations" is that his African American respondents came up with the inverse rank order of discriminations. Myrdal said that, "the Negro's own rank order is just about parallel, but inverse, to that of the White man (Myrdal 1962:61). Myrdal did not see anything concealed in the African American rankings. So, what Myrdal found in both sets of rankings, White and African American, fits very well with Marx's theory of ideology when it is applied to national oppression. The ideology of the oppressing nation inverts reality whereas the counterideology of the oppressed group does not. Here, reality is expressed by African Americans who ranked access to land, credit, jobs, and welfare at the top and barriers to social assimilation at the bottom of their concerns.[2]

Two later studies confirmed Myrdal's findings. Williams and Wiener's (1967) study of African American and White college students found a consistent ordering of discriminations. For White students, intermarriage was at the top of the list just as Myrdal had found. Economic discrimination, however, was not ranked at the bottom. Wilson and Varner's (1973) study of college students also confirmed Myrdal's findings.

CLASS AND THE ASSIMILATION-NATIONALISM SPLIT

Myrdal reviewed evidence of African American nationalism and found that it had no significance. It was clear to him that African Americans really wished only for assimilation and integration and he believed that they knew that could only be achieved with White help. It is also clear that Myrdal saw things only in terms of integration or separation. He had no grasp of the concept of self-determination. Myrdal's rejection of nationalism is interconnected with his class-biased approach to integration. The caste system was blocking the upward mobility of African Americans but the thing that bothered him most was that African Americans who had achieved such things as wealth, education, or property were still a pariah people. This was the greatest contradiction of all with the American Creed for Myrdal.

Harry Haywood, a Marxist, analyzed "Black bourgeois assimilationism" in the 1930s in the following way. It was supported by the "Black bourgeoisie," which was composed of wealthy professionals, businessmen, top educators, local politicians, and so forth.[3] They were to be found in organizations such as the NAACP and the Urban League, which were controlled by White leaders and White money. The Black bourgeoisie were staunchly anti-nationalist. Their power came from the control of the African American press, education, ministerial associations, fraternal organizations, women's clubs, and so forth. They were supported by the White press and they dispensed White patronage. They relied on the bourgeois courts and legislative bodies for reform.

The next class down were the "ghetto petty bourgeoisie" who tended to become "nationalists" in hard economic times with slogans such as "Buy Negro." They depended on the existence of the ghetto market for their livelihood but were also economically limited by segregation. In good times, they were more integrationist. Because neither of these bourgeois classes addressed the interests of working people, utopian, separatist, mass movements such as that of Marcus Garvey grew rapidly in hard times. Often, these movements were just a "hustle." Haywood's hope, of course, was that the rapidly expanding African American working class could be united with the White working class, without ignoring legitimate national-ist demands, and overthrow the capitalist class, including the collabora-tionist Black bourgeoisie (Haywood 1978:428-9).

Haywood's analysis points up the main weaknesses in the integration approach that Myrdal never considered, it could leave millions of African Americans stranded in the wreckage of the ghettos while upwardly mobile individuals were being integrated. The African American nation was not going to be made equal to the White nation, African American individuals would achieve the "American Dream." If we compare this to Lenin's proposal for national self-determination, we see the difference. Lenin called for equal rights for the people of all nations, the end of all special privileges. But in addition, the nations would be made equal. A decent standard of living was not to be contingent on leaving your nation or ingratiating yourself to those from the dominant nation. An improved life could be made within your own nation. On the other hand, a person was free to leave and to expect equal rights outside their own nation. The damage done by centuries of oppression was not to be fixed by destroying the nation, but by building it up.

The integration approach would drive a wedge through the African American nation and split it. Myrdal also said, "the Negro's greatest enemy is the lower class of White people, the people without economic or social security who are competing with Negroes (Rose 1964:27). If the White working class was the greatest enemy to African Americans, their "protec-tors" would be the White bourgeois class as had been the tradition from slavery onward.

As the dismantling of the old apartheid system got underway, the greatest out-break of White nationalism since the Civil War took place across the South. This was followed by an outbreak of African American nationalism that had no precedent.

NOTES

1. Carnegie is famous in labor history as the man who broke the Amalgamated Associa-tion of Iron and Steel Workers. In 1892 at the Homestead Works near Pittsburgh, a plan was

devised to cut wages and end collective bargaining. When the Pinkerton Agency tried to bring in hundreds of strike breakers, a gun battle broke out in which 40 strikers were shot and 9 were killed while 20 Pinkertons were shot and 7 killed. When the surviving Pinkertons surrendered to the workers, they were badly mauled. The state militia was then called out and took control of the plant. After four months, the strike was broken and the union never recovered (Brecher 1962:87-91).

2. Myrdal's assimilation bias explains why he seemed not to see what the African American respondents were saying here. They clearly said that they had little interest in social assimilation but were most concerned with economic matters.

3. Haywood's use of Franklin Frazier's term, *Black bourgeoisie,* should not be confused with what Marx meant when he referred to the "bourgeoisie." The latter consists of the capitalist class, especially large capital, in the White nation. These two "bourgeois" classes are in no sense equivalent because one is, more or less, dependent on the other. Booker T. Washington and Andrew Carnegie are good examples.

REFERENCES

Bennett, Lerone, Jr. 1982. *Before the Mayflower: A History of Black America.* New York: Penguin.

Brecher, Jeremy. 1962. *Strike!* Greenwich, CT: Fawcett.

Caditz, Judith. 1976. *White Liberals in Transition: Current Dilemmas of Ethnic Integration.* New York: Spectrum.

Ellison, Ralph. 1973. "An American Dilemma: A Review." Pp. 81-5 in *The Death of White Sociology,* edited by J. A. Ladner. New York: Vintage.

Halsey, Margaret. 1946. *Color-Blind: A White Woman Looks at the Negro.* New York: Simon and Schuster.

Haywood, Harry. 1978. *Black Bolshevik.* Chicago: Liberator.

Macionis, John J. 1995. *Sociology.* New York: Prentice Hall.

Marger, Martin. 1991. *Race and Ethnic Relations.* 2d ed. Belmont, CA: Wadsworth.

Mead, Margaret. 1946. "Review of Margaret Halsey's *Color-Blind.*" *New York Times,* October 13.

Myrdal, Gunnar. 1962. *An American Dilemma.* New York: Harper and Row.

Pettigrew, Thomas. 1964. *A Profile of the Negro American.* New York: D. Van Nostrand.

Rose, Arnold. 1964. *The Negro in America: The Condensed Version of an American Dilemma.* New York: Harper and Row.

Simpson, George Easton and J. Milton Yinger. 1972. *Racial and Cultural Minorities: An Analysis of Prejudice and Discrimination.* 4th ed. New York: Harper and Row.

Simpson, George Easton and J. Milton Yinger. 1985. *Racial and Cultural Minorities: An Analysis of Prejudice and Discrimination.* 5th ed. New York: Plenum.

Southern, David W. 1987. *Gunnar Myrdal and Black-White Relations.* Baton Rouge: Louisiana State University Press.

Taeuber, Karl E. and Alma F. Taeuber. 1969. *Negroes in the Cities.* New York: Atheneum.

Wellman, David T. 1977. *Portraits of White Racism.* Cambridge, MA: Cambridge University Press.

Westie, Frank. 1965. "The American Dilemma: An Empirical Test." *American Sociological Review* 30:527-38.

Williams, J. Allen, Jr. and Paul L. Wiener. 1967. "A Reexamination of Myrdal's Rank Order of Discriminations." *Social Problems,* Spring:443-54.

Wilson, Warner and William Varner. 1973. "The Rank Order of Discrimination." *Phylon,* March, pp. 30-42.

Woodward, C. Vann. 1962. *The Strange Career of Jim Crow.* New York: Oxford University Press.

6

CIVIL RIGHTS AND
CIVIL UPRISINGS

In the 1960s and 1970s, the Supreme Court played a central role in ending
de jure segregation just as it had in permitting it a half century before.
Congress also participated in dismantling the legal aspects of the apartheid
system. White nationalist reaction to this was protracted and often violent
but it was more or less contained by government action. As civil rights were
being established, however, African American nationalist political struggle
broke loose in a variety of forms, some of it violent and revolutionary in
character. The federal government responded with many new social programs but also with force and often illegal tactics. The Army, FBI, and CIA,
along with local forces, trained and gathered intelligence in preparation for
a civil war.

THE ROLE OF THE COURTS

The Supreme Court "interprets" the constitution and laws passed by Congress very differently at different times as it attempts to help manage
changing sets of contradictions. *Brown v. Board of Education* (1954) is
widely recognized as one of the landmark Supreme Court decisions on
"race." In 1954, the Court ruled that segregated public schools were
unconstitutional. One way to examine this decision is in terms of its
relationship to other Supreme Court race decisions in earlier eras. The

Court has sequentially supported slavery, the end of slavery, segregation, desegregation, compulsory integration, and is currently moving toward the end of compulsory integration.

The Court defended slavery in 1857 in the Dred Scott decision. Dred Scott, a slave, had been taken into a free state, which prompted him to sue for his liberty. He was told by the Court that he could not bring suit because he was property and not a citizen of either the federal government or any state. Chief Justice Taney noted that the constitution had not recognized free African Americans as federal citizens when it was drafted and that many states did not recognize African Americans, slave or free, as citizens. Of course, when Congressional representation was to be determined, slaves were counted as part of the population of each state even though they were not considered citizens. As previously noted, that was part of the deal with the southern states. The constitution assumed that federal citizenship derived from being the citizen of a state (Daniels 1989:272). So Taney concluded that African Americans were not citizens but property. Daniels has suggested that something other than "legal reasoning" influenced Taney (cited in Daniels 1989) when he added to his opinion the statement that African Americans were

> beings of an inferior order, and altogether unfit to associate with the white race, either in social or political relations; and so far inferior, that they had no rights that the white man was bound to respect. (P. 272)

This is a clear statement of evolutionary racist ideology. Taney added it to back up his "legal reasoning." So immediately we see that Supreme Court decisions are not just "reasoned" from existing law. A more creative process goes on even though the Court typically gives great deference in its opinions to the founding fathers and the constitution.

The reasoning is itself important in the Dred Scott case because it illustrates well a key device that has been used repeatedly to allow the oppression of the African American nation, the impotence of the federal government in the face of "states' rights." This, of course, traces back to the writing of the constitution and the politics of slavery. The slave-holding colonies would only agree to form a union on the condition that the federal government not be able to interfere with the right to own slaves. The property owners who created the constitution designed it so that the federal government would be weak in its relationship to private property in general, and especially so with regard to slaves as property. So, for a long time the states outside of the South were powerless to check the slave states as they increased and formed a nation within a nation-state. That southern nation then seceded and tried to conquer what remained of the United States. In reality, then, the United States has been made up of three nations. The federal government was designed in such a way that it could not be used by the nation at large to prevent the oppression of the African American nation held within the White nation in the South.

As we shall see, although much has changed, the South still plays a critical and distinct role in the oppression of African Americans and the federal government still cannot be used effectively to put an end to it.

The Dred Scott decision may have bolstered the ambitions of the South but the Civil War put an end to slavery. The Reconstruction Congress passed legislation to affirm that slavery was ended and to try to end the continuing oppression of African Americans in the South by other means. But, the Supreme Court soon began to interpret these laws in a way that was consistent with what the southern states were doing.

The 14th Amendment to the constitution was one of the most important actions taken by the Reconstruction Congress. It helped overturn the Dred Scott decision. In addition, the amendment tried to address the way in which the South had elected to ignore the Civil Rights Act of 1866 and to reoppress African Americans with their newly passed Black Codes.

Section I. begins as follows:

> All persons born or naturalized in the United States and subject to the jurisdiction thereof, are citizens of the United States and of the state wherein they reside (cited in Lively 1992:48).

This was to establish the citizenship of African Americans as a defense against slavery and other forms of oppression. As we have seen, slavery did not resume but a surrogate for it was created through the sharecropping system. And being a citizen meant little or nothing for African Americans in the post-Reconstruction South.

Another issue should be raised, however, about this amendment. Native Americans, who were not covered by the act, were made citizens by a unilateral act of Congress in 1924 (Falkowski 1992:113). At the same moment that Native Americans became citizens of the United States, they lost the right to be citizens in their own nations. They were not consulted nor did they participate in any way in this decision.

Like Native Americans, African Americans were made the beneficiaries of incorporation into America. Although that was well and good, the Congress was totally blind to the existence of African American people as a nation. African Americans were incorporated only as individuals. Thus, we are left with the thought of what arrangements African American people might have been able to create had they acquired the right of self-determination at the time of Reconstruction. Such a right would have removed African Americans from the power of the southern states and the planter class. Certainly, African Americans would not have knowingly chosen the fate that they were given, nearly 100 years of debt peonage labor on the plantations under the cover of a law that formally made them citizens.

For ideological reasons, we tend not to see what is not covered in the 14th Amendment. The underlying rationale, of course, is that particular identifications such as race are only seen as a barrier to free movement in the free market. By freeing African Americans from their race, through an act in the superstructure, they could then enjoy the freedoms of the "marketplace" in the base of the society. That marketplace turned out to consist of labor contracts leading to debt peonage, prison gang labor, and the like. As Marx noted, it is precisely in the "market" that classes and oppressed nations are formed and reproduced. That which creates oppression, then, is presented as the source of freedom. In the case of the citizen-sharecropper, we have a clear example of extreme inequality in the base being unaffected by a constitutional amendment.

Section I. of the 14th Amendment (cited in Lively 1992) went on to state the following:

> No state shall make or enforce any law that shall abridge the privilege or immunities of citizens of the United States; nor shall any state deprive any person of life, liberty, or property, without due process of law; nor deny to any person within its jurisdiction the equal protection of the laws. (P. 48)

In 1873, the Supreme Court ruled on the meaning of the 14th Amendment. The Slaughter-House case, as it was called, had nothing to do overtly with race but with commerce. Nevertheless, the Court greatly weakened the protections that the amendment might have afforded African Americans. The Court noted that the Amendment had said, "citizens of the United States and of the state wherein they reside." From this wording, the Court found that the Congress had made a distinction between federal and state citizenship, that one citizenship is not the same as the other. Furthermore, the amendment was said to have spoken only to the question of federal citizenship. Therefore, state citizenship was not given additional protection by the amendment, and whatever immunities and privileges might be conferred to a federal citizen were not transferred to the citizen of a state. Similarly, due process was provided for by the constitutions of the states so there was no check or oversight required of the federal government (Lively 1992:70-5). This thinking was extended in the Cruikshank case in 1876. In this case, officials had participated in the massacre of African Americans who had seized a courthouse in Grant parish, Louisiana, in an attempt to defend their right to vote. The massacre was a state matter, ruled the Court. In 1883, a similar ruling in *United States v. Harris* gutted the Civil Rights Act of 1871. The beating to death of a person while in the custody of state officials was ruled to be a state matter, not a federal one. In what were known as the "civil rights" cases, it was ruled that the federal government had no power in instances in which individuals acted against individuals unless such individual actions were sanctioned by the state or done under state authority (Lively 1992:76-7).

The court also ruled that the various Civil Rights Acts and Amendments had the purpose of ending slavery, not of dealing with ongoing discriminations. In other words, the contradictions of the past have been addressed. The new contradictions arising from that resolution could not be addressed by the civil rights laws. Also, in *Virginia v. Rives* (1879), the Court found that all-White juries were of no concern because no state laws required them (Lively 1992:80-4). Just as today, conservatives argue that the modern Civil Rights Acts were to abolish discriminatory laws, not to deal with the existence of discrimination. That is to say, the superstructure exists to correct flaws in the superstructure, not flaws in material, civil society.

With these and many similar rulings, the Supreme Court ratified the reign of terror and segregation that was imposed on African Americans in the South. The federal government rose again to its original state of blindness to African American oppression and let the states do as they would to a defenseless people. By the start of the 20th century, all the southern states had laws requiring segregation of the African American nation from the White nation. And, it should be noted, that many such laws existed in states outside the South.

Segregation was approved by the Supreme Court in the critical case of *Plessy v. Ferguson* in 1896. In this case, a man of mixed-race ancestry was required to sit in the section of a train assigned to African Americans. The court ruled that the seating was "equal but separate." As such, there was nothing invidious implied by the separation, said the Court. A "mere distinction" had been made. Because a state makes distinctions by race, it should not be inferred that it intended to stamp "the colored race with the badge of inferiority" (cited in Lively 1992:91). And the court stated the following:

> If the civil and political rights of both races are equal, one cannot be inferior to the other civilly or politically. If one race is inferior to the other socially, the *Constitution of the United States* cannot put them on the same plane. (Lively 1992:91)

These arguments became the separate but equal legal doctrine that was repeatedly used to support segregation.

As previously noted, segregation was the method chosen, especially by the South, to impress a particularly harsh form of national oppression on the African American nation. All African Americans of all classes were beneath White people of all classes and this was symbolized by physically separating the races at all times in public places. The Supreme Court argued that because the amended constitution gave formal equality to African Americans, they were equal. Being equal in law, separation implied nothing, it said. The fact is, it implied national oppression.

The lesson here is plain for all to see, legal equality can mean absolutely nothing. Legal equality is one thing, equality is something else. Equality is in the material base of society, not in pronouncements made in the superstructure. From a Marxist perspective, when the base changes through its internal contradictions, the particular configurations of inequality change, and then the elements of the superstructure are changed to bring it into conformity with the base. The apparent movement of civil rights law through relatively "progressive" and then reactionary phases can be understood in the relationship of the law to the slave system of production, civil war, and Reconstruction, the creation of the sharecropping system, and then the end of that system.

TOWARD DESEGREGATION

Starting in the 1930s, Thurgood Marshall and the NAACP pursued a strategy of asking the Court to compel the South to make its separate facilities actually equal. After 10 years, in the 1940s there were some modest successes. For example, in 1941 the Supreme Court found the practice of restricting primary elections to White people to be unconstitutional.

In the 1940s, a clandestine program was undertaken to integrate the military services. President Truman issued an executive order to bring this about in 1948. The military kept the changes out of the press as they implemented the order. In the Korean War, which started in 1950, integrated units were used in combat. The integration policy was smoothly and quietly carried out at bases abroad and at home. Woodward (1962) explained as follows:

> Both southern and northern congressmen entered the conspiracy of silence, so that the full import of the new policy did not become generally known until the end of 1953. By that time desegregation was virtually a fait accompli. (Pp. 135-38)

From whom were they hiding this policy of desegregation in the military? The answer must be from the White population in general and especially from the White South. In addition to military desegregation, some African Americans had been enrolled in a number of the previously segregated universities in the South without much difficulty (Woodward 1962:135).

In 1950, however, the Supreme Court ruled decisively against segregation in graduate education and the South began to react. Thurgood Marshall had targeted graduate education because most southern universities had no separate facilities for African Americans. In *Sweatt v. Painter,* the Court ruled that a hastily created "law school" was not equal to established law schools. On the same day, it ruled in *McLaurin v. Oklahoma* that the practice of physically segregating a student within a White graduate school impaired the ability to learn (Woodward 1962:130).

In a panic after this decision, the South began to pour millions of dollars into African American educational facilities. It also launched a crash program to build public toilets, drinking fountains, athletic facilities, and roads for African Americans (Woodward 1962:146). But it was all to no avail. In 1954, the Supreme Court ruled against the separate but equal doctrine.

There is overwhelming evidence that the framers of the 14th Amendment had no intention of causing schools to be integrated (Lively 1992:110). Nevertheless, the Supreme Court said that it could not determine what the original intent had been with regard to schools. Instead of legal precedent in this area, the Court relied on data from social science studies that had been introduced by the NAACP to assert that equal protection was denied when schools were segregated. Separation denotes inferiority, which affects the ability of African American children to learn, said the court, and thus, "separate educational facilities are inherently unequal" (Lively

1992:112). Gunner Myrdal's entire study was cited in a footnote to the *Brown* opinion (Southern 1987:229).

The *Brown* decision specifically overturned *Plessey v. Ferguson,* which had said that separate but equal facilities involved no violation of the 14th Amendment. This was clearly a step forward. The *Brown* decision said, however, that there could be no such thing as "separate but equal schools."

Both the *Plessey* decision and the *Brown* decision were talking about segregation, which is not synonymous with "separate." As previously noted, over a century ago Switzerland recognized the existence of four, equal, internal nations. Children of these nations have attended separate but equal schools ever since. Other consociational societies with separate school systems include Belgium, The Netherlands, Canada, Yugoslavia, and the USSR before the collapse of communism. The use of the term *separate* by the Supreme Court has contributed greatly to a profound ideological distortion of the entire debate about race in this country. People equate the southern apartheid, segregation system with all forms of separate existence of peoples. This ignorance has ideological roots. It helps explain the position of many liberals who, in their sincere commitment to ending racism, are so certain that the only possible solution to the "race problem" is the color-blind disappearance of African Americans into White America. To be sure, White nationalists of the old school would look on any suggestion of separate national existence with great joy. But the support of White nationalists would quickly turn to reaction once they understood what the equality and self-determination of nations would actually entail.

The Supreme Court would have used entirely different language if it had followed a course of establishing equal rights for African American individuals by striking down all segregation laws and at the same time recognizing the existence of the African American nation. Instead, all reform was hammered through the "equal rights" channel, whether it fit or not. This was a strategy that has perpetuated White national hegemony in a new form.

THE SOUTHERN REACTION

The *Brown* decision was aimed directly at the South. It was the South that was an international embarrassment. Former Secretary of State Dean Rusk (Blackstone and Heslep 1977) recalled that

A Black ambassador could drive his family down to a beach in Maryland for a weekend and be turned away. An ambassador to the United States, of dark color, [was refused service at a Miami airport]. . . . It was very difficult for Blacks to know where they could have a meal in our national capital. (P. 155)

Initially, the *Brown* decision did not cause too much reaction because the Court assumed that a policy of gradualism would eventually bring about cooperation from the southern states. But, by 1956, it became clear that the Court would require compliance. White Citizen's Councils had been forming all across the South. Violence against the NAACP occurred and one person was killed. Klan-inspired rioting erupted at the University of Alabama in 1956, which eventually produced the expulsion of an African American student who had enrolled there. Senator Harry Byrd from Virginia, along with hundreds of other politicians, called for "massive resistance" to school integration.

As resistance picked up, Chief Justice Earl Warren, the Supreme Court, Gunnar Myrdal, the Carnegie Corporation, and sociology in general were denounced in the White South as Communist. William F. Buckley, Jr. "red baited" Myrdal in a 1957 editorial in the *National Review,* while Arnold Rose was attacked as a Jewish Communist (Southern 1987, chap. 7).

The easy successes in military and university desegregation may have given the impression that desegregation in general would not be difficult. If there were illusions about this, they were shattered when the issue became public school desegregation. Both class inequality and national inequality in the base of society are preserved by the structure of unequal education in the superstructure. Then as now, the wealthy, who send their children to private schools or who use public schools in exclusive communities, are basically immune from the effects of desegregation. But the *Brown* decision attacked the advantaged position of White working-class school systems. When the initial action was taken against southern schools, the resistance was violent and fanatical.

In 1957, President Eisenhower had to send soldiers from the 101st Airborne Division to safely escort nine African American students to a Little Rock, Arkansas, high school. After this event, many legal strategies were devised to avoid, evade, or delay school integration. Private schools spread rapidly and some were funded with public money. "Freedom-of-choice" plans, gerrymandering of district lines, and school closure were all attempted. In addition, riots, school burnings, and murder were used to resist school desegregation.

De jure segregation existed where state laws required it. These laws were struck down by the Supreme Court in 1954. By 1961, seven years after the *Brown* decision, five southern states had still not integrated any public schools (Pohlmann 1990:40). Eventually all the states did integrate public schools to some extent but de facto segregation, segregation as the result of residential segregation, continues to be a major source of segregation to this day. By comparison, the desegregation of public facilities in the South was quite successful and complete.

THE CIVIL RIGHTS MOVEMENT

Aldon Morris (1984) has analyzed the role of various "half-way houses" in the civil rights movement. These were typically White or partially multiracial, egalitarian, activist organizations that had no mass base but that had a great deal of knowledge about movement organizing and the techniques of social change. The Highlander Folk School, for example, located in the mountains of Tennessee, was founded by Myles Horton, a working-class White man. The school was involved in union organizing in the 1940s and it organized both White and African American workers, arguing that Whites and African Americans had a common enemy, the rich (Morris 1984). The school was often vilified as a "training school for communists." In fact, it attracted a variety of people, from Marxists to religious reformers. Prominent movement leaders such as Martin Luther King, Rosa Parks, James Bevel, and so forth, attended meetings at Highlander (Morris 1984).

The African American church also played a critical role in the movement. Franklin Frazier (1963:43) has referred to "the church as a nation within a nation." Exiled from the politics of the White nation, much of African American political life has taken place in the local as well as the nationwide structure of these churches. Those half-way houses that promoted passive resistance and nonviolence as moral techniques of social change found common ground with African American churches and their Christian doctrines of nonviolence and love of one's enemies.

The "Jim Crow" laws, which were the hallmark of the sharecropping era, were brought down by a campaign of civil disobedience, which eventually forced the Congress to act. Brutal attacks on passive protesters before television cameras produced a national and then international outcry against the South. The bus boycott in Baton Rouge in 1953 and the Montgomery bus boycott in 1955; the sit-ins in Greensboro, North Carolina, in 1960; the Freedom Rides on interstate buses; and the Birmingham demonstrations were part of a vast social movement that swept across the South. The Department of Justice reported 1,412 demonstrations in just three months of 1963 (Zinn 1995:447). Beatings, tear gas, water hoses, dogs, jails, and fines were all used against the protesters. In 1963, Martin Luther King gave his famous "I Have a Dream" speech to a quarter of million people gathered in Washington, D.C.

It was in the summer of 1964 that three young civil rights workers—two White, one African American—were murdered in Mississippi by Klan-connected law officers and others. Those who had organized the civil rights effort had earlier asked President Johnson and Attorney General Kennedy for federal protection but had gotten no response (Zinn 1995:447-8). The perpetrators were acquitted by an all-White Mississippi jury. Later, they were convicted for violating the civil rights of the victims under a federal statute. Thus, in these new times, the federal government found a way to get around "states' rights" and get a conviction for murders of national oppression.

In 1964, another Civil Rights Act was passed by Congress. Title VII made discrimination in employment illegal. It had previously been made illegal by the Civil Rights Act of 1866 and 1871 (Edwards 1977). Title II of that act prohibited discrimination on account of race in hotels, motels, restaurants, gasoline stations, and places of amusement if their operations affect interstate commerce or if their actions are supported by state actions (cited in Simpson and Yinger 1972:462). When we note that the Civil Rights Act of 1875 prohibited discrimination in "accommodations, advantages, facilities, and privileges of inns, public conveyances on land or water, theaters and other places of public amusement" (cited in Lively 1992:78), we must ask what was the difference between 1875 and 1964? How could the same institution in the superstructure pass essentially the same law twice, the first time having no effect and the second time having a permanent effect? A Marxist would say that federal law is associated with the end of Jim Crow laws in the South in the 1960s, and not before, because the sharecropping relations of production, which produced Jim Crow laws, were over by then and not before. We also see again that the Congress had to invent a special device, "interstate commerce," to intervene in the internal affairs of the states. This invention, like the use of social science in the *Brown* case, took the place of legal precedent. So it came to pass that foreign ambassadors would soon be able find accommodations wherever they went in the South and African Americans could enjoy what the White public enjoyed—if they had the money.

Title I of the 1964 Civil Rights Act dealt in a very weak way with voting discrimination in the South. The Voting Rights Act of 1965 abolished poll taxes, limited literacy tests, and forbid intimidation. Most important, it provided for federal examiners, the Attorney General, and federal courts to intervene where violations occurred. The effect on African American voting was dramatic. In 1964, 38 percent of African Americans in the 11 southern states were registered to vote. By 1968, it was 62 percent (Simpson and Yinger 1972:393).

Some African Americans, however, found that these civil rights were too far removed from their actual lives to affect any meaningful change.

ALL HELL BREAKS LOOSE

The revolutionary potential in the African American population, which Marxists like Lenin and Haywood had long ago foreseen, suddenly began to explode in the 1960s. As Marx observed in the case of Irish oppression, although national division retards class struggle in the working class of the dominant nation, the combination of national and class oppression makes revolutionary activity more likely among the workers of the oppressed nation.

A new type of "race riot" was first seen in 1964 in Harlem and then in 14 other cities, mainly in the northeastern United States (Allen 1970:28). Prior to this, all race riots in the United States were initiated by Whites and were directed against African American lives and property. These were pogroms of national oppression, which had the purpose of either terrorizing resident African American populations or driving African American people completely away from White-held communities. The new race riots were African American uprisings directed mainly against White-owned property in urban ghettos and against the police (Graham and Gurr 1969; Button 1978).

Robert Allen (1970:28)has said that African Americans "were in a sense 'reclaiming' the merchandise that had been stolen from them in the form of underpaid labor and exploitive prices." These uprisings were not in any sense revolutions, but they had an element of revolutionary logic to them. African Americans by the tens of thousands took control of their communities by violence and seized the valuable possessions of White property owners. Other than the uprisings following the murder of Martin Luther King in 1968, almost all of these events were triggered by conflict between the local police and African Americans. During the uprisings, the police were the main targets of interpersonal violence by African Americans. Police are not just police to many African Americans—they are more like an army of occupation. Across the contradiction of race, they represent the sharpest point of national oppression. To this day, there is a tendency for some police officers to beat or shoot African Americans of all classes, a holdover from the days of Jim Crow-style national oppression.

The Watts uprising, which occurred in 1965, was one of the biggest of the period. Like many such events, the trouble was precipitated by conflict with the police. A traffic arrest of a young African American turned into a scuffle between police officers, the family of the person arrested, and then a crowd that had gathered. Police clubbed a woman in the crowd. The uprising sparked by this incident lasted for three days and three nights. Thirty-four people were killed, most of them African Americans. Hundreds of people were injured. Mobs assaulted White motorists, firemen, and journalists but none was killed. Police were the main target of assault throughout the uprising. Ninety were injured but none of them was killed. At the peak, 1,653 officers were deployed (Oberschall 1967:325). But at times the police were forced to withdraw from the streets. Property damage was set at $40,000,000. Four thousand people were arrested. Order was restored when 13,900 National Guard troops were used to enforce a curfew (Oberschall 1967:325).

Button (1978) reported that there were 329 important uprisings between 1964 and 1968. Downes (1968), looking at 239 incidents, found that there were close to 50,000 people arrested, 7,942 wounded, and 191 killed during this period of time. Massive events took place in Newark and Detroit with a total of 83 dead. In the first six months of 1968, there were 131 urban uprisings, most of them resulting from the murder of Martin Luther King (Allen 1970:126).

The uprisings, which were spontaneous, took place almost entirely within African American communities and some of them never fully recovered from the destruction of businesses and homes. Political organizations did not produce these riots nor did they lead to much political organizing. The White pogroms of the earlier era killed thousands of African Americans. The African American uprisings described here resulted in the death of about 200 people, and almost all of them were African Americans who were killed by the police and soldiers. Enormous amounts of revolutionary energy were dissipated by these uprisings. Looting commodities is a far cry from taking control of the means of production.

REVOLUTIONARY AFRICAN AMERICAN NATIONALISM

There is a long history of African American nationalist movements and organizations in the United States. In the 1960s, however, there was an extraordinary revolutionary nationalist upsurge. Unquestionably, Malcolm X was the most influential "Black" nationalist of the period. His father had been a member of Marcus Garvey's separatist organization, UNIA. One of the earliest memories of Malcolm X was of his home being burned down by racists. His father was later murdered by racists. As a young man, he engaged in many criminal activities and spent many years in prison. While in prison, he became a member of the Nation of Islam, a nationalist, separatist organization that arose from the lower class of the African American nation (Haley and Malcolm X 1966). Commenting on the uprisings in 1964, Malcolm X (cited in Blair 1977) said,

> 1964 will see the Negro revolt evolve and merge into the worldwide Black revolution that has been taking place on this earth since 1945. The so-called revolt will become a real Black revolution. . . . Revolution is always based on land. Revolution is never based on begging somebody for an integrated cup of coffee. Revolutions are never fought by turning the other cheek. Revolutions are never based on love-your-enemy and pray-for-those-who-spitefully-use-you. And revolutions are never waged singing "We Shall Overcome." Revolutions are based upon bloodshed. . . . Revolutions are never even based upon that which is begging a corrupt society or a corrupt system to accept us into it. Revolutions overturn systems. And there is no system on this earth that has proven itself more corrupt, more criminal, than this system that in 1964 still colonizes 22 million African Americans, still enslaves 22 million Afro-Americans. (P. xvii)

The revolutionary Black nationalist movement was an inversion of the integrationist movement. The two sides of this contradiction were defined by class differences. The leadership of the integrationist movement consisted of "bourgeois" African Americans who worked in an alliance with certain bourgeois Whites. Color-blind ideology and integration fit this alignment of class and national interests. As Haywood (1978) noted, however, the bourgeois class within the African American nation is in no way the equal of that of the White nation, but is a dependent class. The situation of working-class and poor Whites and African Americans is different. Although they have common class interests, these are overridden by national divisions and competition, which pit one against the other and produce polar nationalist impulses in both.

The urban uprisings of the 1960s inspired an entirely new type of Black nationalism that challenged bourgeois African American leadership. Malcolm X, in particular, articulated a brilliant counterideology that exposed and infuriated the integrationist leaders.

In 1964, Malcolm X devised a plan to charge the United States before the United Nations with violating the human rights of the African American nation. In his speeches, he pointed out that virtually all of the colonies that had gained their independence had adopted a socialist economy. He advised African Americans to consider doing the same thing (Allen 1970:37).

In 1965, Malcolm X broke with the Nation of Islam and started his own organization. He had traveled widely in the previous year and his views had changed significantly. The Nation of Islam did not participate in politics. It condemned all White people as the Devil and asked for a separate state in which all African Americans could live. Malcolm X wanted to organize a politically active, all-African American organization that might work in alliance with a certain kind of White organization. He was amazed by the great number of White people who wanted to join his organization or have him speak to their churches or organizations. He told them that if they wanted to fight racism they should do so in their own communities, where it originated. Perhaps one of his greatest contributions was the way he explained the necessity of achieving the right of self-determination for a people who had been so cruelly and destructively subjugated. People saw in him a profound dignity and self-respect. Malcolm X was shot to death while speaking at a public meeting in 1965 by several African American men who may have been associated with the Nation of Islam (Haley and Malcolm X 1966:367).

In the summer of 1967 in the aftermath of the Detroit uprising, Bayard Rustin, a long-time civil rights leader, said that the rioting had to be stopped with whatever force was necessary. He said that if the rioting continued the established civil rights leadership would be devastated. Control would pass into the hands of destructive leaders in the ghettos ("What Can be Done?" 1967:31). The NAACP, the Urban League, Martin Luther King, and A. Philip Randolph all agreed that force had to be used to stop the riots ("An American Tragedy" 1967:25).

President Johnson had sent 4,700 paratroopers to Detroit where they joined National Guard units and police in attacking the riot areas. Patton tanks and Huey helicopters were deployed. A reporter observed a tank firing at a brick building for 25 minutes. A family of four was found under the back porch with no weapons. National Guard troops fired wildly at "anything that moved" ("An American Tragedy" 1967:25).

In Detroit, as in many of the uprisings, there were many reports of "snipers" but few, if any, were ever found. There were also many who believed that some organization somehow caused these events to happen, but no evidence of this was ever found. Former-President Eisenhower said he was terrified of the riots and that they must have been planned ("What Can be Done?" 1967:31).

The Kerner Commission was created in 1968 to study the ghetto uprisings along with other forms of violence in America. It attributed the uprisings entirely to "White racism" (see Graham and Gurr 1969:788-821). It would not be expected, of course, that such a commission would understand Malcolm X's perspective and see that the uprisings were something created by an oppressed nation.

CO-OPTATION AND CONTROL

By the mid-1960s, a number of integrationist civil rights leaders began to adopt a more nationalist rhetoric in response to the criticism they had encountered from Black nationalists. A number of liberal organizations such as CORE adopted the Black Power slogan. Cultural nationalism in the form of African hair styles and dress became very popular.

The "War on Poverty" was developed by President Johnson in 1964 under the OEO (Office of Economic Opportunity). OEO initiated such things as the Job Corps, Youth Corps, Head Start, Vista, Legal Services, and CAP (Community Action Program). A number of the programs, especially CAP, enabled a significant number of African American activists to be put on the federal payroll. Similarly, the Ford Foundation, headed by McGeorge Bundy, changed its race programs from philanthropy to funding grants for antipoverty projects in a number of cities.

Public housing was established in the Roosevelt era as temporary assistance to the poor. By the mid-1960s, 50 percent of the units were occupied by African Americans. A variety of programs were initiated to get them out of public housing but at the same time Housing and Urban Development (HUD) embarked on its massive "Urban Renewal" plan. From coast to coast, thousands of "blighted" neighborhoods were bulldozed. African Americans called it "Negro Removal" (Button 1978). At best, HUD was a mixed blessing to African Americans.

The NAACP, the Urban League, and CORE received various kinds of grants from the Ford Foundation. Top leaders such as Roy Innis, Andrew Young, and Martin Luther King received Ford-funded fellowships. The

Black Power Conference in 1967 in Newark was attended by 1,300 African Americans from 190 organizations. Unknown to most, it was funded by some 50 American corporations. Although many themes were present, a determined effort was made to channel Black nationalism into "Black capitalism" at the conference. (Allen 1970, chap. 4).

In 1968, in endorsing "Black capitalism," Richard Nixon (quoted in Allen 1970) stated the following:

> It's long been common practice among many to draw a distinction between "human rights" and "property rights," suggesting that the two are separate and unequal—with "property rights" second to "human rights." But to have human rights, people need property rights—and never has this been more true than in the case of the Negro today. (P. 228-9)

In other words, Nixon conceded that the granting of legal civil rights was not enough. "Property rights" were needed too and Black capitalism would do that. The question, of course, was what would Black capitalism do for African Americans who were not Black capitalists but African American workers? Allen (1970) documents numerous programs undertaken by corporate America as a result of the ghetto uprisings. From Allen's perspective, these were designed to bring the ghettos under the control of a new African American elite class, which would in turn be controlled by the White ruling class. In other words, it was to be a vast expansion of the old Andrew Carnegie-Booker T. Washington relationship.

REVOLUTION

Conversely, the ghetto uprisings gave a number of African Americans and some White people, too, the thought that a revolution could actually be made in the United States. The Black Panther Party undoubtedly made the most serious efforts in this direction. The Panther party was founded in Oakland in 1966. It called openly for revolution and for the use of weapons for self-defense. The Panthers did effective organizing in ghettos across the country around issues such as police brutality and hunger.

The Student Nonviolent Coordinating Committee (SNCC) was an activist civil rights organization that worked in the South. Its members came mainly from middle-class backgrounds. In 1966, Stokely Carmichael, a SNCC leader, first articulated the "Black Power" slogan on the James Meridith March in Mississippi. Martin Luther King, also on the march, rejected the slogan. The slogan, however, was subsequently adopted by many activists and civil rights organizations despite its vague meaning. In 1967, an attempted alliance or merger between the Black Panthers and SNCC failed. Alliances were also attempted between the Panthers and the Students for a Democratic Society (SDS), a White campus activist organization, and with the Peace and Freedom Party. Common ground was found on issues of opposition to the Vietnam War and university campus issues such as the establishment of Black Studies programs and departments (Sale 1974). But alliances between White and African American organizations were tenuous at best.

By the 1970s, a number of White college students and a few African American students who had been "radicalized" by civil rights and anti-Vietnam War experiences, attempted to create new communist parties. Two key problems for all of these new parties were how to unite with African American people and how to unite with the working class. Hundreds of students left their colleges and universities to take factory jobs or other working-class jobs. They soon discovered that the contradiction between White workers and African American workers was even more difficult for them to deal with than the one that split the middle class of the United States (Sale 1974; Davidson 1972). In response to this, they developed theories that ranged from a "pure class struggle" (in other words, color-blind theory) to theories that, in some way, recognized the separate existence of African American people. These parties more or less died out by the mid-1980s. One of them, the Communist Workers Party (CWP) was attacked by Klansmen and Nazis in Greensboro, North Carolina, in 1979. Five CWP members or supporters were shot to death (Bermanzohn and Bermanzohn 1980).

REPRESSION

Repression of the African American nation had primarily been a southern task for most of this country's history. Local authorities handled the problem crudely but effectively for 200 years. But with the mass migration of African Americans out of the South and into urban areas, North and South, repression was no longer a regional problem, it literally became a national problem.

The federal government responded to the ghetto uprisings, "Black" revolutionary nationalism, and also the White student movement as if preparing for a civil war. The U.S. Army began extensive troop training to deal with the problem. A 24-hour "domestic war room" was set up at the Pentagon staffed by 150 people. A thousand soldiers in plainclothes infiltrated political groups. Intelligence files were developed on every known activist in the country (Button 1978). The FBI developed its own intelligence files while the CIA, illegally, did the same thing. The Law Enforcement Assistance Act (LEAA) was created in 1968 to strengthen local police. Millions of dollars went for increased pay, expanded forces, training, gas, arms, helicopters, armored cars, intelligence gathering, and so forth (Button 1978).

The Black Panthers were subjected to especially blatant police repression. In 1969, two Panther leaders, Fred Hampton and Mark Clark, were killed when police stormed their apartment in an early morning raid. Around the country, Black Panthers were killed, jailed, or went into exile to survive. By 1972, "most militant Black leaders were either in jail, had left the country, or had gone 'underground.' " (Button 1978:138).

Something of the extent of government repression during the previous decades became known in 1971 when someone broke into FBI offices in Media, Pennsylvania. They stole files that documented the activities of the Counter Intelligence Program (COINTELPRO) and released them to the newspapers (Wise 1976:281). Eventually, Congress passed the Freedom of Information Act, which required a limited release of these files. The identity of those involved was withheld so that no one could ever be prosecuted for what they had done and a great deal of information was withheld (Wise 1976). Nevertheless, it became clear that every activist African American group had been targeted for infiltration and many had been subjected to activities designed to harass, split, or destroy them. The same was true of every organization on the White left. It was obvious that a vast network of informers and agents existed throughout the country.[1]

By the end of the 1970s, the movement, as it was called, was dead. With the election of Ronald Reagan in 1980, a period of reaction set in that continues to this day.

NOTE

1. It recently came to light that Supreme Court Justice Thurgood Marshall had repeated contacts with the FBI during this period. The FBI noted Marshall's great concern that Communists had joined the NAACP. Marshall passed on information to the FBI about Robert Williams, a North Carolina NAACP member who advocated armed self-defense. He also

sought information from the FBI about Black Panther demonstrations against him ("FBI File" 1996).

REFERENCES

Allen, Robert L. 1970. *Black Awakening in Capitalist America.* New York: Doubleday Anchor.

"An American Tragedy." 1967. *Newsweek,* August 7, p. 25.

Bermanzohn, Paul and Sally Bermanzohn. 1980. *The True Story of the Greensboro Massacre.* New York: Cesar Cauce.

Blackstone, William T. and Robert D. Heslep. 1977. *Social Justice and Preferential Treatment.* Athens: University of Georgia Press.

Blair, Thomas. 1977. *Retreat to the Ghetto: The End of a Dream?* New York: Hill and Wang.

Brown v. Board of Education, 347 U.S. 483 (1954).

Button, James W. 1978. *Black Violence.* Princeton, NJ: Princeton University Press.

Daniels, William J. 1989. "The Constitution, the Supreme Court, and Racism: Compromises on the Way to Democracy." *National Political Science Review* 1:126-32.

Davidson, Carl. 1972. "Lessons from the Collapse of the Communist Party (Marxist-Leninist)." Unpublished manuscript.

Downes, Bryan T. 1968. "Social and Political Characteristics of Riot Cities: A Comparative Study." *Social Science Quarterly* 49:504-20.

Edwards, Harry T. 1977. "Race Discrimination in Employment: What Price Equality?" Pp. 71-144 in *Civil Liberties and Civil Rights,* edited by V. J. Stone. Urbana: University of Illinois Press.

Falkowski, James E. 1992. *Indian Law/Race Law: A 500-Year History.* New York: Praeger.

"FBI File: Marshall Sought Help from Agency in 1950s." *Virginian-Pilot,* December 3.

Frazier, Franklin. 1963. *The Negro Church in America.* New York: Schocken.

Graham, Davis Hugh and Ted Robert Gurr. 1969. *Violence in America: Historical and Comparative Perspectives.* New York: Bantam.

Haley, Alex and Malcolm X. 1966. *The Autobiography of Malcolm X.* New York: Grove.

Haywood, Harry. 1978. *Black Bolshevik.* Chicago: Liberator.

Lively, Donald E. 1992. *The Constitution and Race.* New York: Praeger.

McLaurin v. Oklahoma State Regents for Higher Education, 339 U.S. 640 (1950).

Morris, Aldon. 1984. *The Origins of the Civil Rights Movement.* New York: Free Press.

Oberschall, Anthony. 1967. "The Los Angeles Riot of August 1965." *Social Problems* 15:322-41.

Plessy v. Ferguson, 163 U.S. 537 (1896).

Pohlmann, Marcus D. 1990. *Black Politics in Conservative America.* New York: Longman.

Sale, Kirkpatrick. 1974. *Students for a Democratic Society (SDS).* New York: Vintage.

Simpson, George Easton and J. Milton Yinger. 1972. *Racial and Cultural Minorities: An Analysis of Prejudice and Discrimination.* 4th ed. New York: Harper and Row.

Southern, David W. 1987. *Gunnar Myrdal and Black-White Relations.* Baton Rouge: Louisiana State University Press.

Sweatt v. Painter, 339 U.S. 631 (1950).

United States v. Harris. 106 U.S. 629 (1883).

Virginia v. Rives, 100 U.S. (10 Otto) 313 (1879).

"What Can be Done?" 1967. *Newsweek,* August 7, p. 31.

Wise, David. 1976. *The American Police State: The Government Against the People.* New York: Vintage.

Woodward, C. Vann. 1962. *The Strange Career of Jim Crow.* New York: Oxford University Press.

Zinn, Howard. 1995. *A People's History of the United States: 1492-Present.* New York: Harper Perennial.

7

THE COLOR-BLIND REACTION

NEW TIMES, NEW IDEOLOGY

The southern economy is no longer dependent on a labor system of sharecropping and debt peonage. The system of legal segregation, which arose from that base and sustained it, has been destroyed. The ideology of evolutionary racial differences, which sustained the old system, has been discredited—although attempts to revive it do occur. Arthur Jensen's (1973) *Educability and Group Differences* and Richard Herrnstein and Charles Murray's (1994) *The Bell Curve* are two examples. Both books argued that the tendency of African Americans to score lower than Whites on IQ tests was indicative of innate differences in intelligence between the two races. Both books attracted a great deal of attention for a time after they were published. But the outcome was the same—liberals heaped scorn on the books, conservatives did not want to be associated with them, and they were, more or less, forgotten. Today, evolutionary "racist" ideology cannot become the dominant, articulated ideology. An unknown number of people still believe what it says is true but only a very few will openly subscribe to the ideology. Evolutionary racist ideology is incompatible with the new patterns of "race relations." Whether it is foreign or domestic affairs, one cannot espouse doctrines of innate superiority of White people when "integration" characterizes a significant part of the interaction between the White nation and nations of color. Nevertheless, national oppression and inequality continue, so it is predictable that ideologists would be hard at work constructing a new ideology concerning "race."

Twenty years ago, Sidney Willhelm (1976) observed the following:

> Throughout its history, White America adjusts its expression of racism to accord with its economic imperatives and modifies its myths of racism to take into account the shifting economic circumstances . . . White America generates a new ideology to sanction any fundamental alteration in race relations growing out of basic economic modifications. (Pp. 155-6)

The new ideology is "color blindness." Denying the existence of the African American is not new, as has been shown, it was made an integral part of the constitution by the founding fathers. What is new is that it became the dominant ideology when it replaced evolutionary racist ideology. As noted, it was started in the 1950s as a liberal ideology promoted by integrationist elites. Then, in the 1970s, it was transformed into a conservative ideology using only part of Supreme Court Justice Harlan's 1896 argument for a color-blind constitution. This, in turn, became the legal rationale for reversing or undermining key liberal programs such as affirmative action, voting rights, and school integration. "Reverse discrimination" became the battle cry of legions of White voters who became Republicans, and then of the Clinton "New Democrats," who concluded that the only way to defeat the Republicans was to become indistinguishable from them.

CONSERVATIVE VERSUS
LIBERAL COLOR-BLIND IDEOLOGY

Conservative color-blind ideology capitalizes on the oppressive elements that are inherent in the notion of color blindness even when it is used by liberals. This is the reason liberals have not been able to mount much defense against their opponents. The roots of color-blind ideology are found in the classic liberal doctrines of freedom—the freedom of the individual created by the free capitalist marketplace. Because liberals and conservatives are both defenders of capitalism, the differences that exist between them disappear as you go to the common root of their ideologies, the free marketplace. For liberals, the government may intervene in some elements of the operation of the marketplace to make capitalism work better. Sometimes that means responding to the demands of the oppressed. Conservatives are opposed to most liberal efforts that would favor the oppressed. Conservatives, then, are much more inegalitarian than liberals. In the case of race, they claim that government intervention is unconstitutional, immoral, and racist because the government is not color-blind. Government intervention actually makes the realization of a color-blind society impossible, they say.

It should be noted that conservatives are not, however, opposed to government intervention in the marketplace that favors the rich. The recent disaster of the savings and loan institutions illustrates this whole issue quite well. These institutions were deregulated in the name of marketplace freedom. What followed was wild speculation and outright fraud, which led to the failure of many of these institutions. At least 326 billion dollars of federal tax money were used to cover the losses (Blackwell 1991:103). Many industries receive government subsidies in one form or another and often appeal for government help when they are in trouble.

Both conservatives and liberals condemn race reactionaries, people such as Klan members, and all those who subscribe to evolutionary racist ideology, although the condemnation from conservatives is comparatively rather muted. Conservatives also agree with liberals in condemning the segregation laws of the Jim Crow period when the federal government condoned state laws that segregated Whites from African Americans. At that time, the government acted in a racist way and this was wrong, say the conservatives. All of this was corrected by the establishment of equal civil rights and that was where things should have stopped. Liberals, however, took things much farther than that. Liberals used government to try to bring about the equality that only the free marketplace can bring. It is precisely this point that liberals cannot answer. They cannot formulate an answer to the conservatives without questioning this key element of capitalist ideology: the belief that freedom derives from the capitalist marketplace. Liberals will not say that oppression is inherent in the marketplace. If the free marketplace did not create the systems of slavery, sharecropping, and the urban ghetto, what then is left? If "racial" oppression does not come from the base of society, it has to come from the superstructure. It must have arisen from the government, the main enemy of the marketplace and freedom. Caught in this way, liberals cannot defend their government policies very well at all.

Affirmative Action as Affirmative Discrimination

Nathan Glazer wrote one of the first books setting forth the conservative arguments against the liberal agenda in 1975. He attacked what he called "affirmative discrimination" in the areas of employment, busing in education, and in housing. He concluded with chapters on the "ethnic backlash" and on the immorality of affirmative action. Glazer reviewed the Civil Rights Act of 1964. He noted that again and again it used phrases such as "no discrimination on the grounds of race, color, religion, or national origin." Glazer (1975) called particular attention in Title VII of the Act to 703 (j), which reads as follows:

> Nothing contained in this title shall be interpreted to require any employer . . . to grant preferential treatment to any individual or to any group because of the race, color, and so forth. (P. 44)

Glazer then noted that during debate on the bill, all sides agreed that "racial balance" was not to be required of employers by way of "quotas" (Glazer 1975:45).

Research shows that the majority of Whites support affirmative action if it is called just that. If it is called or linked to the terms "preferential treatment," "quotas," or "reverse discrimination," the majority of White people do not support it (Harris 1996:328). In the political arena, a great debate has ensued over these terms. Liberals deny that the terms really describe affirmative action. Conservatives say that the terms are accurate and they are contrary to the express wishes of Congress in the Civil Rights Act of 1964. The Supreme Court, it seems, tried to find a middle ground in this debate in 1978 in the *Bakke* decision. The Court forbid the University of California to reserve a proportion of admissions only for African Americans. But the Court stated that the university could give points, so to speak, for race when determining admissions. This *is* a preference if not a fixed quota. It is a preference designed to overcome the historic and continuing preference given to White males.

Thus, the conservatives seem to have the letter of the law on their side when they fight against "preferential" treatment. If affirmative action does ignore the law on race, this is nothing new. Most of Reconstruction civil rights law was ignored or reversed. But why was affirmative action created? President Kennedy was the first to use the phrase "affirmative action," but it meant little more than "out-reach" to minorities in hiring. It was not very different, then, from what President Roosevelt did in 1941 in ordering the end of discrimination in defense industries, or Truman and Eisenhower in banning discrimination on the part of government contractors.

In 1965, however, President Johnson gave a speech at Howard University in which he stated the following:

Freedom is not enough. You do not wipe away the scars of centuries by saying now you're free to go where you want and do as you desire and choose the leaders you please. You do not take a person, who for years has been hobbled by chains, and liberate him, bring him up to the starting line of a race, and then say, you're free to compete with all the others, and justly believe that you have been completely fair. . . . It is not enough to just open the gates of opportunity. All our citizens must have the ability to walk through those gates.

This is the next more profound stage of the battle for civil rights. We seek not just freedom but opportunity . . . not just equality of right as a theory, but equality as a fact and a result. (Johnson quoted in Eastland and Bennett 1979:6)

Terry Eastland, a prominent conservative race ideologist, traces the origins of preferential treatment to the Equal Employment Opportunity Commission (EEOC), which was created in 1965. Alfred Blumrosen, one of EEOC's officials, began the practice of inferring discrimination from the employment records of companies. According to Eastland, Blumrosen used evidence of statistical imbalances to pressure employers to hire African Americans. In addition, in 1965, Johnson's Executive Order 10925 placed affirmative action in federal contracting under the Office of Federal Contract Compliance (OFCC). That office began the practice of awarding contracts based on pledges to employ a workforce with "proportional representation" of minorities (Eastland 1996:48-9).

It is generally acknowledged that President Johnson took these extraordinary steps because of the threat of urban riots. Laws against discrimination were not enough, employers had to be compelled to take affirmative action.

The basic problem can still be seen today. An incident in 1994 involving senior Texaco executives was recently revealed. It illustrates the difficulty in detecting and proving discrimination, and thus the continuing necessity of affirmative action. At a meeting to plan a response to a discrimination lawsuit, Texaco executives used many racist epithets while conspiring to destroy records. One of the executives secretly tape-recorded the meeting. After he was "downsized" in 1996, the executive turned the tape over to the plaintiffs in the case ("On Tape, Texaco Officials Talk" 1996). This rare exposure shows not only what can go on at the highest level of corporate

America, but the near impossibility of it ever coming to light. The basic method of affirmative action is to look at the composition of a particular company's workforce relative to the available, qualified workforce. If there is a significant discrepancy, the company is required to take some remedial action. To date, a better method has not been found.

Terry Eastland (1996) grants that the riots were what motivated President Johnson to launch affirmative action, but he argues that this should not have happened and would not have happened if the riots had been correctly interpreted. He states the following:

> The *interpretation* placed on the inner-city race riots of the 1960s confirmed the turn in elite opinion. The traditional *response* to a riot had been to hold the rioting individuals responsible for their actions, but that did not happen in this case, because the riots were seen as a necessary, and even just, response to what Whites had done to Blacks historically. (P. 44, emphasis added)

The elites that Eastland talks about here are "the civil rights establishment and . . . political liberals" (Eastland 1996:44). He suggests that these elites did not hold the rioting individuals responsible. As we saw in the previous chapter, however, this is not the case. The civil rights "elites" condemned the rioters and called for their suppression. Bayard Rustin saw the riots as a threat to established civil rights leadership. But, the same leaders also argued that the riots were the result of oppression.

When Eastland talked about the "traditional response" to rioting, he gives the impression that modern-day rioters were not held accountable for their actions. In truth, the traditional race riot was a White nationalist pogrom and the traditional response to the traditional pogrom was to do little or nothing to the Whites who carried out these mass murders. On the contrary, law officers and government officials often participated in the attacks or facilitated them. In contrast, as we have seen, the police and military attacks on the ghettos produced about 50,000 arrests, many wounded, and many killed. African American individuals were held accountable, some were brought to trial, some were shot down in the streets, and a type of collective punishment was administered to residents of the ghetto.

President Nixon, the conservative Republican president who followed Johnson as president, expanded affirmative action. This fact put Terry Eastland in a very difficult position. Was Nixon a closet liberal? Eastland (1996) gave two reasons why President Nixon expanded affirmative action.

First, according to Eastland, Nixon's memoirs showed that he wanted to "drive a wedge" between African Americans (NAACP) and unions (AFL-CIO), both of whom were supporters of the Democratic party. Second, he wanted to do something to prevent more riots. To these ends, he implemented what was called the "Philadelphia Plan" for most major cities. The plan required construction workers' unions, employed on federally funded projects, to hire African American apprentices with the possibility of getting union membership when they became qualified. Also, in 1969 Nixon created the Office of Minority Business Enterprise (OMBE) by executive order. The office disbursed 100 million dollars to minority businesses. These "set-asides" were Nixon's contribution to "Black capitalism." Also, under Nixon, Hispanics (including Cubans), Asians, American Indians, and women were brought in as protected categories. In 1972, Nixon denounced the use of quotas. He also sent clear messages to the South that he was opposed to busing for school integration and he tried but failed to weaken the Voting Rights Act.

Nevertheless, Eastland, a conservative Republican, was forced to criticize not only President Johnson, the liberal Democrat, for capitulating to rioters, but President Nixon, a fellow conservative Republican. The position of Eastland is very much like that of the conservatives who call President Roosevelt a "traitor to his class." Such conservatives cannot accept the idea that Roosevelt's creation of things such as Social Security, his "socialism," helped save American capitalism during the crisis of the Great Depression. President Johnson was a liberal from the Roosevelt era. Like Roosevelt, he was facing a crisis that threatened American capitalism. Affirmative action was the equivalent of a little dose of socialism to ward off something worse. But President Johnson receives no accolades from Terry Eastland for dealing with the African American uprising in the urban ghettos, nor does the archconservative, Richard Nixon. In the beginning, the use of affirmative action was a bipartisan affair, which tells us that at the time the ruling class was united in using this measure to try to bring things under control. It came to be perceived, however, as a liberal, Democratic policy because Republicans soon turned against it, at least in their rhetoric.

But why is affirmative action so offensive to conservatives? It recognizes race, they say. But *race* is a term that ideologically disguises *nation*. What the liberals are really saying, whether they know it or not, is that to effectively bring the African American nation under control, they had to weaken it, split it, and disperse it. To do that, they had to recognize, in some way, that it existed. The conservatives are opposed to this strategy and so is a significant part of the White nation. Liberals argue that they must exercise temporary race consciousness to arrive at the goal of a color-blind society. Someday, African Americans will be so thoroughly dispersed throughout White America that no trace of them as a people will remain. Race will have no meaning and all concerned will be color-blind. This was the liberal plan. It was not unlike President Lincoln's vision of the dispersal and colonization of the freed slaves.

Conservatives do not oppose this but maintain that the process must not be accelerated by the government with affirmative action. It must take place naturally, so to speak, through the marketplace, even if it takes much longer. Here, one suspects that the objective is to hold the African American nation in color-blind limbo forever. Both the liberal and the conservative plans employ color blindness to oppress the African American nation—the liberal to dissolve it, the conservative to maintain it as an oppressed nation. Part of the liberal crisis arises now from the fact that it appears that the African American race cannot be dissolved.

Justice Harlan's Blindness

Segregation law, like modern liberal law, implicitly recognized the existence of the African American nation under the disguise of race. In the environment of evolutionary racist ideology, state laws recognized race and contributed to the ways in which the White nation could maximize its advantage over the African American nation. The post-Reconstruction Supreme Court negated the first Civil Rights Acts and permitted the states to do this using a variety of arguments, especially the "separate but equal" argument.

After the battle to save segregation law was lost, the modern conservatives arose to condemn any law that recognized race. Nathan Glazer's (1975) book was the first to lay out this line of argument. He stated it was wrong for courts to order the busing of students from one district to another to achieve racial integration. States should not have segregated schools by law, and states should not integrate them either—this is the de jure/de facto distinction. Segregation laws should have been eliminated, but if integration did not result after the laws were gone, it was not the business of the state to compel integration. The same was true of the use of affirmative action in employment. Although Glazer approved of the 1968 Act prohibiting discrimination in housing, he was not sure what role the government might play to prevent the inner-city, African American/suburban, White split that was already well advanced.

Glazer (1975) noted that resistance to what he called "affirmative discrimination" was very difficult because the civil rights movement had the "moral" high ground. At the same time, he noted the power of the growing "White backlash." He attributed this to the "ethnic" identification of the Whites involved. Thus, Glazer suggested that Polish Americans, Irish Americans, and so forth were reacting against the civil rights movement out of something like an ethnic reflex. This ethnic explanation was a rather transparent cover for blue-collar White nationalism. In truth, everybody who came from Europe to America became a "White" person relative to African Americans. Glazer's (1975) ethnic argument was an attempt to somehow equate the nationalism of the oppressed African American nation with the nationalism of the oppressor White nation. They are, however, not the same thing. The former is a nationalism of liberation, the latter is the opposite.

Conservatives saw a great potential in the White "backlash" for drawing the White working class away from the Democratic party and into the Republican party. To do that, they had to develop a moral argument that could compete with those of the civil rights movement and, at the same time, avoid any identification with evolutionary racist ideology. The pioneering work on this was done by Terry Eastland and William Bennett (1979) in their book titled *Counting By Race*. Glazer had mentioned in passing that Justice Harlan had stated that the constitution was "color-blind" in his dissent in the *Plessy v. Ferguson* (separate but equal) case. Eastland and Bennett built much of their legal and moral argument around part of Harlan's dissent:

> In view of the constitution, in the *eye of the law,* there is in this country no superior, dominant, ruling class of citizens. There is no caste here. *Our constitution is color-blind and neither knows nor tolerates class among citizens.* In respect of civil rights, all citizens are equal *before the law.* The humblest is the peer of the most powerful. The law regards man as man, and *takes no account* of his surroundings or of his color when his civil rights are guaranteed by the supreme law of the land. (Harlan cited in Eastland and Bennett 1979:83, emphasis added)

This is what Eastland and Bennett (1979) cited from Harlan's dissent. They omitted, as have all their conservative comrades, the beginning of the paragraph, which says the following:

The *white race* deems itself to be the *dominant race* in this country. *And so it is,* in prestige, in achievements, in education, in wealth, and in power. *So,* I doubt not, *it will continue to be for all time, if it remains true to its great heritage and holds fast to the principles of constitutional liberty.* (Harlan cited in Hofstader and Hofstader 1982:58, emphasis added)

Eastland and Bennett (1979) omitted this but they follow what it prescribes exactly. *It says that the best way to maintain the domination of the White nation is to follow the color-blind constitution in all matters of law.* Harlan, a former slave owner, felt that the "separate and equal" argument was a subterfuge that permitted the public degradation of an inferior people (Lively 1992:92-4). To him, it was a gratuitous degradation but, more important, it was one that weakened the whole society by degrading the state, the bourgeois state.

Harlan offered some critical advice. The White nation should never seek explicit, overt help from the state to maintain its dominance. On the contrary, the law must be as pure as the driven snow. The law (capitalist law) knows nothing of classes or races in society. The law provides "constitutional liberty" to all individuals regardless of class or race.

Yes, as Marxists would explain, it provides constitutional liberty, but not liberty. The constitution is blind to class and national oppression although classes and nations exist and operate in the base of society. Bourgeois law made the law blind to the existence of class and nation to preserve and protect both forms of inequality. The blind constitution is an inversion of the material world, which has its eyes wide open.

Harlan tried vainly to instruct the Court in the fundamentals of capitalist law. Failing to understand, the Court implicitly acknowledged the existence of both the White and the African American nations in the guise of race. Harlan clearly despaired at such incompetence.

At certain times the contradictions in the base of society force the ruling class to take the state and use it vigorously to adjust the structure of class and national inequality to prevent chaos or revolution. Liberal theorists then offer such events as proof of the autonomy of the state, that the state is driven by ideals, and that it is independently capable of opening its eyes to injustice. Of course, it may be hard to explain to the skeptic just why law is blind at one time and sighted at another. Eastland argued that the constitution is blind so the state must be blind at all times. Urban uprisings and the threat of revolution were no excuse for then-Presidents Johnson and Nixon to create a way for the federal government to invade the base of society and deliberately alter the structure of national oppression and inequality. Clearly, the whole liberal/ conservative debate is focused on the line of contradiction that delineates the base of society from the superstructure. But the debate itself is driven by the contradictions in the base.

Glazer (1975) started the process of flipping the liberals on their ideological heads with the concept of affirmative discrimination. Eastland and Bennett, more or less, completed the task. Justice Harlan said that the law cannot take race into account. Thus, affirmative action programs are actually racist because they take "race into account." Eastland and Bennett (1979) said that Harlan's view is the proper way to understand the concept of equality. It should be called *moral equality*. Moral equality means that "every person should be considered as an individual, not as a member of some racial or ethnic group to which he belongs or says he belongs" (p. 9). In contrast, there is *numerical equality,* which has to do with proportional representation of groups. This leads to reverse discrimination, which is equivalent to regular discrimination. One thing is as immoral as the other and neither is constitutional. The inversion is thus complete, Whites are victims, not African Americans. In this way the color-blind conservatives came to believe that they had wrested the moral high ground from the civil rights "establishment" and the liberal elite. Conservatives, then, have a moral obligation to carry out a just, populist, struggle against liberal racists. To see race is racist. All of society must turn a blind eye to race, especially the law. By this logic, we find people asserting that the NAACP is a racist organization because it is not color-blind. Similarly, we are told that Klan-type racists have been replaced by liberals who stigmatize African Americans by identifying them by their race to subject them to affirmative action. African Americans, so labeled, are looked down on by Whites who would have otherwise welcomed them into schools and jobs. To justify their opposition to affirmative action, conservatives are fond of saying that it is they who have inherited the mantle of Martin Luther King, who advocated a color-blind society. They say this despite the fact that King endorsed affirmative action.

The list of conservative intellectuals who subscribe to color-blind race ideology has grown rapidly. A few of the better known, in addition to Terry Eastland and William Bennett, include William F. Buckley, James Kilpatrick, Chester Finn, George Will, Nathan Glazer, Daniel Moynihan, Lee Rainwater, Seymour M. Lipset, Edward Banfield, Ben Wattenburg, Clint Bolick, and Charles Murray. African American conservatives such as Thomas Sowell, Shelby Steele, Alan Keyes, Stephen Carter, Walter Williams, Robert Woodson, and Armstrong Williams play a special role. Their endorsement of color blindness gives the ideology greater legitimacy by blurring the two sides of the contradiction. Dinesh D'Souza, from India, and Linda Chavez, a Hispanic, have played essentially the same role.

Gamson and Modigliani (1987) traced how the attack on affirmative action was "framed" and disseminated through television, news magazines, editorial cartoons, and opinion columns. Initially, affirmative action was framed as "remedial action" during the Johnson and Carter years, but was reframed as reverse discrimination during the Reagan years. Gamson and Modigliani identified journals such as *The Public Interest, Public Opinion,* and *Commentary;* think tanks such as the American Enterprise Institute and the Hoover Institution; and organizations such as the Coalition for a Democratic Majority as sponsors of articles, books, and legal briefs promoting the framing of affirmative action as reverse discrimination. They traced the dissemination of this framework through the press and television networks. They found that these ideas "resonated" among those White people who sought to defend traditional racial inequalities and they adopted them.

THE ROTATION OF POLITICAL PARTIES AROUND NATIONAL AND CLASS CONTRADICTIONS

As noted previously, President Nixon's writings showed that he saw affirmative action as a way to split working-class Whites away from the Democratic party by using the threat of job competition between African Americans and unionized White workers. This is a good example of race being used as a political "wedge." This political strategy goes back to abolition politics in the way in which the Southern planter class broke up the Populist movement in the post-Reconstruction period. As we have seen, working-class Whites united with the White capitalist class to protect their race interests, but ultimately it was at the expense of their class interests.

We recall that those African Americans who could vote generally voted Republican from the end of the Civil War up to World War II. The White working class tended to vote Democratic throughout this period so the "racially" split working class voted in two different parties. The Democrats blamed the Republicans for the Great Depression, labeled them the "party of the rich," and enjoyed much electoral success. The policies of Roosevelt's "New Deal" changed African American voting behavior, particularly the policy of providing federal employment for African Americans. At the time, this had little or no effect on White voting in the one-party, Democratic South. In the election of 1948, Harry Truman's support for civil rights may well have made the difference in his victory. African American voters, now living in Northern cities in significant numbers, cast votes that tipped the scales to the Democrats (Polenberg 1983). When he became president, Truman opposed lynching, the poll tax, and created the Fair Employment Practices Act (FEPA). His administration justified their promotion of civil rights for African Americans using the familiar anticommunist rationale. Polenberg (1983) noted, however, that conservatives, especially Southerners, turned the connection between civil rights and anticommunism into a "boomerang." Liberals had essentially argued that America at least had to do as well as the communists with regard to oppressed internal nations. Conservatives argued that equality between the races was a communist idea. In truth, as we have seen, foreign and domestic communists had taken the lead in support of racial equality. The Southern conservatives argued then, that real anticommunists should oppose racial equality. This is another example of conservatives creating a paradox by inverting liberal ideology.

When the Democratic party adopted a strong civil rights plank in 1948, the "Dixiecrats" bolted the party. Strom Thurmond, then governor of South Carolina, headed the State's Rights Democratic party. In his campaign, Thurmond said that "reds" and "subversives" had captured the Democratic party, and that civil rights had "its origin in communist ideology," and that its real purpose was "to excite race and class hatred" (Polenberg 1983:110).

The Dixiecrat phenomenon revealed the possibility of breaking the hold that the Democratic party had on what was called the "Solid South." The same thing was demonstrated in 1964 when Barry Goldwater was soundly defeated by Lyndon Johnson. Goldwater won the Republican nomination as a result of a right-wing takeover of the party. The "Eastern Elites," the old guard of the party that supported civil rights, lost out to the Goldwater faction (Edsall and Edsall 1991).

Both the Democratic and the Republican parties have a "liberal" and a "conservative" wing. The liberal wing of both parties tends to derive from big capital, which is internationally oriented. The Eastern Elites of the Republican party were sometimes called "Rockerfeller Republicans." As we have seen, liberal elite advocates of racial integration, such as Myrdal and his circle, frequently expressed great concern about international relations. The conservative wing of both parties is more provincial, both economically and politically. For example, it tends to oppose membership in the United Nations. Of course, the core of the conservative wing is located in the South—the South, which remained largely agrarian until the post-World War II period (see Kerbo 1991:210-25 for a general discussion of upper-class rule).

One person who conservatives often refer to when they attack the liberal elite is McGeorge Bundy. Bundy, the president of the Ford Foundation in the 1960s, was born into "a rich Boston Brahmin family" (Lind 1996:164). He was a graduate of Groton and Yale. His father was a partner in an elite Boston law firm. As Special Assistant for National Security Affairs during the Johnson administration, Bundy was one of the principal architects of American strategy in the war in Vietnam. As head of the Ford Foundation, Bundy was active in trying to turn "Black nationalism" into "Black capitalism." In 1977, Bundy published a frequently cited article in the *Atlantic Monthly* titled "The Issue Before the Court: Who Gets Ahead in America." In the article, he argued that racially neutral admissions policies to colleges would produce very little results. He supported preferential treatment and said race had to be taken into account to get beyond race (Bundy 1977:45). Thus, Bundy provides a good example of an upper-class elite who played an important role in promoting the use of racial preferences.

From this perspective, the entire dispute between liberal integration and conservative laissez faire desegregation reflects a split within the ruling class that corresponds to the division between big, international capital and smaller, regional capital. As we have seen, something similar existed over the abolition of slavery and the Civil War. The Democratic party split in two, North and South, over expansion. This enabled the new Republican party to elect Lincoln. Northern capital grew rich off the war and expanded the powers of the federal government in a way that reflected its new dominance. So, it was this faction of the ruling class, big industrial capital, that led the way in resolving the contradiction between the development of industrial capital and the slave-labor system in the South by first resisting the expansion of slavery and then abolishing slavery and winning the Civil War.

Thus, it could be argued that in the contemporary period, it was big, internationally oriented capital that proposed to resolve the postsharecropping race crisis with the strategy of integration. Initially, the strategy of this left wing of the ruling class was represented by the left wing of both the Republican and Democratic parties, but the Goldwater campaign showed the right wing of the Republican party the potential to be had in racist reaction, in other words, in the realm of small and provincial capital, especially in the South.

Goldwater was a classic antigovernment conservative. He was one of the few in Congress who had voted against the 1964 Civil Rights Act. In the campaign, he supported the elimination of school segregation laws but opposed the use of busing to bring about integration. Goldwater was the first Republican since Reconstruction to carry any states in the Deep South. He won five of them. But outside the South, he only carried his home state of Arizona.

Research showed that poor Whites in the South had begun to shift from Democratic to Republican voting. Although previously they had been highly supportive of liberal Democratic policies on economic issues, this was overridden by their reaction to the civil rights movement. In fact, by the 1970s poor Whites no longer supported liberalism on economic issues (Edsall and Edsall 1991:41). In other words, they had come to the position of voting against their own economic class interests hoping to protect their race interests.

President Johnson steamrollered the Southern segregationist wing of the Democratic party as he pushed the Great Society legislation through Congress and helped move the agenda from civil rights to "equality of outcome." At the same time, the liberal, Warren-led Supreme Court reinforced the "rights revolution" that was underway. Strom Thurmond, the old Dixiecrat, and Jessie Helms, the archconservative, became Republicans (Marable 1995:83). In 1968, George Wallace, the former governor of Alabama and staunch segregationist, running as an independent, pulled millions of former Democratic voters away from Hubert Humphrey, and helped President Nixon win the election. Wallace won virtually the same Southern states that Thurmond and Goldwater had won before him (Edsall and Edsall 1991:79). Ken Phillips (cited in Edsall and Edsall 1991), a key Republican strategist, wrote in 1969:

Maintenance of Negro voting rights is essential to the GOP. Unless Negroes continue to displace White Democratic organizations, the latter may remain viable as spokesmen for Deep Southern conservatism. (P. 81)

So, just as Nixon advanced affirmative action, Phillips advocated voting rights. All, for the purpose of splitting the White South and the White worker in general away from the Democratic party.

In the wake of defeat in Vietnam and the Watergate scandal, the Democrat from Georgia, Jimmy Carter, beat Gerald Ford in the 1976 presidential election. He carried the South because of the African American vote but he failed to win the votes of the majority of White Southerners (Carmines and Stimson 1989:246).

Nevertheless, the Republican "southern strategy" came to full fruition with the election of Ronald Reagan in 1980 and his reelection in 1984. Lee Atwater (cited in Edsall and Edsall 1991), campaign manager for Reagan said the following: "In the 1980 campaign, we were able to make the establishment, in so far as it is bad, the government. In other words, big government was the enemy, not big business" (p. 145). In other words, the Democrats had flourished since the Depression by hanging the tag of "establishment" on big business. Now that Democrats were using government to push integration, the Republicans could make government the establishment and the enemy. But this was only possible because of the appeal to White nationalism that was disguised as an "antigovernment" campaign. It had to be disguised because open appeals to White nationalism had been discredited.

The Republican party platform in 1980 (cited in Edsall and Edsall 1991) endorsed nondiscrimination and stated the following:

> However, equal opportunity should not be jeopardized by bureaucratic regulation and decisions that rely on "quotas," ratios, and numerical requirements to exclude some individuals in favor of others, thereby rendering such regulations and decisions inherently discriminatory. (P. 144)

Thus, the color-blind position became part of the platform of the Republican party. In addition to reverse discrimination, Reagan attacked crime in the streets, welfare, fair housing legislation, busing for integration, and government in general. He supported state's rights, gun ownership, and law and order.

Lee Atwater advised George Bush in the 1988 campaign. In this campaign, Atwater employed one of his most criticized political ploys. Atwater discovered that, as governor, Dukakis had furloughed from prison "Willie" Horton, an African American convicted of murder. While on rehabilitation furlough, Horton raped a White woman and assaulted her husband. The Bush campaign frequently used a photo of the assailant in television ads that attacked Dukakis's liberalism.

AFRICAN AMERICAN MAJORITY
VOTING DISTRICTS

Swain (1995) argued that in 1991, 60 percent of the African American population was in the South and that reverse migration (from North to South) was continuing. But, she noted that only 20 percent of the African Americans in Congress come from the South. Most African Americans in Congress come from cities with a population greater than 300,000 and there are few of these in the South (Swain 1995). So, the majority of African Americans who were located in the South had very poor political representation in Congress.

The Voting Rights Act of 1965 was amended by Congress in 1982 so that African Americans and other minorities could sue to have discriminatory voting districts redrawn so that they would comprise a voting majority within the new districts. In 1986, in *Thronburgh v. Gingles,* the Supreme Court held this practice to be constitutional.

Redistricting was promoted strongly by the Bush administration after the 1990 census. Lee Atwater had seen a way in racial redistricting to increase Republican electoral victories. If African Americans were removed from districts in which they were a minority and packed into a new, single district, the loss of these Democratic-voting African Americans from their previous districts could give the Republicans the edge in elections. To this end, the Republican party created a private foundation to assist African Americans and Hispanics in creating new districts in which they would be the majority. In addition, the Justice Department in the Reagan and Bush administration worked with African American state legislators in selected states to bring about racial gerrymandering (Lind 1996:175).

African American majority districts increased from 17 to 32 while Hispanic districts increased from 9 to 20. In 1992, the Congressional Black Caucus had 29 members (Lind 1996:174). The Democratic party was well aware of what the Republicans were trying to do. In the four southern states where they controlled redistricting, they tried hard to carve out African American majority districts in a way that would protect Democratic majority districts. The result was often an unusually extended, barely contiguous, majority African American voting district. In the 1992 elections in these four states, the Republicans neither gained nor lost seats. In the 1994 elections they gained seven new seats, but, taking a conservative estimate, only three of them might have been the result of redistricting (Lublin 1995:121). In the five southern states where Democrats did not control the redistricting process, Republicans gained nine seats, with six or seven of them due to redistricting changes. Republicans gained six more seats in the 1994 election but that is not attributed by Lublin (1995) to the earlier redistricting. African Americans gained 13 seats in this process but this was somewhat offset by the 9 seats gained by Republicans. Any African American advantage was nullified by the fact that Republicans gained a total of 22 seats by 1994. White liberal Democrats who held 49 percent of the seats from these states in 1990, held only 23 percent after the 1994 elections. For the first time in 40 years, the Republicans won a majority in both houses of Congress. According to Lublin (1995), it was not redistrict-ing per se that accounted for the Republican victory in 1994, but redistrict-ing made the difference in giving Republicans the majority of seats. Lublin observed that African Americans had gained "descriptive" representation while losing "substantive" representation (Lublin 1995:111-22). Michael Kelly (1995), writing in *The New Yorker,* has suggested that the Republi-cans caused even more damage to the Democrats than the loss of Congres-sional seats. First, Kelly cites Charles Bullock, a political scientist, who argues that the Democrats managed to operate as a biracial coalition by not acknowledging race (Kelly 1995:46). Then, Kelly quoted Benjamin Ginsberg, a Republican involved in the redistricting scheme, who sug-gested that the alliance of Republicans and African Americans created a serious feeling of mistrust between Democrats and African Americans (Kelly 1995:48). Kelly noted that the Democratic party might become a mainly African American party in the South. In fact, the White South is now predominantly Republican, White voters outnumber African Ameri-cans by 6 to 1, and the South contains 54 percent of the electoral votes needed to elect a President (Kelly 1995:48).

This Republican redistricting strategy was another case of the party promoting civil rights to make their party the party of the White nation in the South. It worked—the White South again is the region that drives the politics of the White nation at large. It is quite remarkable that the party that made color blindness a moral principle promoted African American majority voting districts for this purpose. The fact that this "southern strategy" worked is *prima facie* evidence of the existence of a White nation in the South. The Democratic party's nonracial, color-blind politics (mainly that African Americans support White, liberal Democrats) were no match for the Republican party's shrewd manipulation of African American nationalist impulses and the underlying White nationalism that made the whole thing possible.

Of course, the Republican party's identification as the "White" party has won them many White votes outside the South, too. This attests to a White national consciousness that exists from coast to coast.

THE SUPREME COURT
GOES COLOR-BLIND

Voting Districts Attacked

The success that the Republican party had in electing presidents over the past 25 years gave them the opportunity to appoint enough conservatives to the Supreme Court to transform it from a majority liberal court to a majority conservative court. Their greatest victory in this regard was the appointment of Clarence Thomas, a "color-blind" African American. Thomas replaced Thurgood Marshall, the only other African American to ever serve on the Court. The other four conservative justices are Sandra Day O'Connor, Anthony Kennedy, and Antonin Scalia. They all subscribe to the ideology that the law must be color-blind and not take race into account when fashioning remedies for racial discrimination.

In 1993, in *Shaw v. Reno,* the Court held for the five White appellants from a newly created African American majority district in the state of North Carolina. The appellants' complaint was

> the deliberate segregation of voters into separate districts on the basis of race violated their constitutional right to participate in a "color-blind" electoral process. (*Shaw v. Reno* 1993)

Sandra Day O'Connor noted in her opinion that even though the appellants invoked Justice Harlan's color-blind constitution, they acknowledged that there might be some circumstances in which the state might not be color-blind. O'Connor agreed with them that this is true and noted that their complaint was not based simply on color blindness but also on the "irregularity" of the district that had been drawn (*Shaw v. Reno* 1993).

The fact was that this district in North Carolina was one that had been drawn by Democrats and was designed to protect their interests. This was the reason for the extreme irregularity. (Apparently the district was extremely long and narrow to spread the loss of African American voters over many districts.) O'Connor argued that the district was so irregular that it must have been drawn for the purposes of segregating the races. It was unconstitutional, then, under the Equal Protection Clause of the 14th Amendment (*Shaw v. Reno* 1993). By a vote of 5 to 4 the Court sent the case back to the North Carolina courts.

This is some of Justice O'Connor's color-blind reasoning. Express racial classifications are suspect because there is no way to know if they are "benign" or motivated by racial politics. Such classifications are "odious to a free people whose institutions are founded upon the doctrine of equality" (*Shaw v. Reno* 1993). "Assignment by race may serve to stimulate our society's latent race-consciousness" (*Shaw v. Reno* 1993). For the state to take race into account there must be a compelling government interest and "close scrutiny" must be exercised. (Close scrutiny essentially amounts to a ban.) The district in question resembles "apartheid." And O'Connor wrote the following:

> Racial classifications of any sort pose the risk of lasting harm to our society. They reinforce the belief, held by too many for too much of our history that individuals should be judged by the color of their skin. . . . Racial gerrymandering . . . may balkanize us into competing racial factions. (*Shaw v. Reno* 1993)

The Court's decision is truly a color-blind one. It has a vision of what politics must be. A person who "happens to be African American" can be elected to office. But no African American person can be elected to office for the purpose of representing African American people. African American people as such can have no representation. They do not exist but such districts might cause them to exist. To recognize race is immoral and racist.

Liberals have difficulty answering this because they hold that the color-blind disappearance of the African American is the proper outcome of what they are doing. Liberals concede the point that race should disappear. They can only argue that their "pluralism" is a means to that end. But why should a race have representation?

The only way to answer the color-blind disfranchisement of African American people, whether it is liberal or conservative, is to say that African American people are an oppressed nation. As such, they have the right of self-determination, which includes the right of political autonomy or political representation. Color blindness presents a choice of two types of national oppression. The conservative gives no representation, and the liberal gives a dependent, indirect, quasi-representation.

One of the main points made by the four Justices who dissented from the *Shaw v. Reno* (1993) decision was that there is nothing wrong when the state acts to correct a situation in which a "minority" lacks political representation. Such an act is not the same thing as what the majority does when it discriminates. In other words, the oppressor and the oppressed are not equivalent. "Equal protection" cannot mean that they be treated as the same thing. It was further argued by the dissenters that the irregularity of the district in question did not reveal some secret. The state was openly trying to respond to the requirements of the Civil Rights Act of 1965 as amended in 1982. To do so it had to take race into account (*Shaw v. Reno* 1993).

Following the Supreme Court's ruling, courts in Georgia, Louisiana, and Texas began to rule that African American majority voting districts were unconstitutional primarily because they were not compact. In Georgia, one of three such districts was redrawn leaving it about one third African American in population.

When the federal court in North Carolina reheard the *Shaw v. Reno* (1993) case, it did not change its original ruling. It let the district stand as drawn. So, in 1996, the Supreme Court ruled on it again along with a similar case from Texas. The same five Justices ruled that both districts were unconstitutional for essentially the same reasons given previously.

In June 1996, a panel of Republican-appointed federal judges in Texas redrew 13 districts. They threw out the results of primary elections and ordered new ones. In North Carolina, a panel of three judges decided that redistricting could wait for legislative action next year. Two of the three were appointed by Democrats ("Texas Districts Redrawn" 1996).

So, it appears that the effect of the court's color-blind rulings will be to force many of the African American majority districts to be dissolved or drawn in such a way that Democratic districts undergo further decline. Either way, African American political representation will be greatly reduced.

Affirmative Action Under Attack

In addition to attacking African American majority voting districts, the conservative Court has followed a strategy of whittling down affirmative action. When the Court was more liberal in 1980, it held that it was constitutional to allocate a sum of public works money for minority-owned firms in *Fullilove v. Klutznick.* But in 1989 in the *City of Richmond v.*

Croson, the Court ruled against setting money aside for minority firms. In this case, the African American majority city council in Richmond, an African American majority city, found that less than one percent of the city's construction contracts went to minority contractors. They set aside 30 percent for that purpose. By a six-to-three majority, the Court said this violated the Equal Protection Clause and that any use of racial classification by a government agency should be subjected to "strict scrutiny." It also said that mere statistical imbalances did not prove that discrimination had occurred. In 1990, the Court seemed to reverse itself in *Metro Broadcasting v. FCC,* saying that it could distinguish between "benign" and "invidious" racial classifications. After that decision, two liberals retired from the Court and were replaced by conservatives. In 1995, in *Adarand v. Pena,* the Court basically reiterated what it had said in *Croson.* In this case, it said that the federal government discriminated against Adarand, a White person, in promoting the awarding of contract to a company headed by a Hispanic. Justice Clarence Thomas, in the majority, of course, said that "these programs stamp minorities with a badge of inferiority and may cause them to develop dependencies or to adopt an attitude that they are 'entitled to preferences' " (Thomas quoted in Eastland 1996:141).

A skeptic might point out that veterans serving in the military from 1944 to 1976 and in wars thereafter have received extra points on civil service exams. It appears that no stigma attached to them, despite the boost they received in hiring. Similarly, children of alumni of many universities, athletes, and children of wealthy donors get extra "points," so to speak, in college admission decisions. Yet they seem not to wear a badge of inferiority or develop attitudes of dependency.

Although this "badge of inferiority" thesis is commonly asserted as a fact by conservatives, I am unaware of any actual research that has even tested the idea that African Americans who have received preferences in hiring or college admissions have experienced psychological harm.

There are creditable studies showing that affirmative action does produce results in the hiring of minorities and women. Pincus (1994) reviewed several studies that used the same design. These studies compared firms that were covered by affirmative action regulations to those that were not covered. All of the studies found that, in the covered firms, the employment of minorities and females grew significantly faster than in the firms that were not covered. Hacker (1995:124) noted that many firms act on their own to increase minority employment rather than risk legal action or bad publicity. In other words, the mere existence of affirmative action regulation moves firms to act.

Resegregating Schools

The Court has also moved against school desegregation. In 1991 in the Oklahoma City case, the Court ruled that because the city had complied with court orders to end de jure segregation and had implemented busing plans to integrate its schools, it had a "unitary" school system. As such, it was free from additional court supervision. It was also free to end busing for integration because the segregation that would result was caused by residential (de facto) segregation, something for which the school board was not responsible. In his dissent, Justice Thurgood Marshall said, "The majority today suggests that 13 years of desegregation is enough" ("Excerpts from Court Decision" 1991).

A number of cities have followed the example of Oklahoma City. Gary Orfield (quoted in Wicker 1996:96), a specialist in school desegregation, commented in 1995 on this movement, "It's real, it's large, and it's threatening to get us to a level of segregation we haven't seen since before the civil rights movement." Orfield reported in 1992 that, nationwide, public schools had become more segregated than they had been in 1967 (Wicker 1996:96).

In addition to contributing to the resegregation of the public schools, these decisions by the Supreme Court mean that African Americans will get fewer government contracts and the underrepresentation of African Americans in Congress will get worse.

Blind Law, the Key to Class and "Race" Domination

In the decisions reviewed previously, the Supreme Court referred frequently to the 14th Amendment to the constitution in these rulings, which states as follows:

> No state shall make or enforce any law which shall abridge the privileges or immunities of citizens . . . nor deprive any person of life, liberty, or property, without due process of law; nor deny to any person within its jurisdiction the equal protection of the laws. (quoted in Hofstader and Hofstader 1982)

So, the 14th Amendment is consistent with the color-blind constitution. It recognizes only individuals and forbids the states to treat people unequally. In a number of these contemporary rulings, the Court cited Justice Harlan who said that the constitution is color-blind. Of course, the Court did not cite Harlan when he also said that the White race would forever remain dominant if it would stick to color-blind law. How does this work?

As Harlan said, the Court must be able to say that all are equal before the law. And Anatole France said, "The law in its majestic equality forbids the rich as well as the poor to sleep under bridges, to beg in the street, and to steal bread" (quoted in Lenski 1996:52). Thus, when a poor person is arrested for sleeping under a bridge, the law can say that it sees this person as only a person and neither as a rich nor a poor person. The poor are the equal of the rich before the law. This means two things, the law has no class prejudice and the law will be applied to individuals as individuals abstracted from any facts of their social existence such as class or race. Thus, the law can say to the poor, and to the rich, if a rich person is ever brought before this court for sleeping under a bridge, they too will be sent to jail. Furthermore, if rich White people ever burn and loot their own gated communities, suburban malls, and country clubs, we will shoot them down like dogs and hold them individually responsible for their actions.

Bourgeois law is predicated on the great, preposterous, fiction that unequals are equal. Statutes of blind justice adorn courthouses everywhere. They are an unquestioned and revered part of the ideological culture that supports this fiction.

Harlan tried to warn that there is a grave danger when the law admits to the existence of race and class—even to oppress. If it is allowed that race and class exist, the law might someday be used to take into account the class and race existence of individuals brought before the court. The poor cannot be allowed to sleep under bridges because they are poor. The next thing would be the poor sleeping in beds that are not their own. The ultimate "absurdity" would occur if the working class or the poor began to file class action suits to bring about equality. If bourgeois law admitted to the existence of race and class and really began to take them into account, bourgeois society would collapse.

Under the extraordinary conditions that existed following the breakup of the sharecropping system and the resulting threat of revolution, bourgeois law recognized the existence of the African American nation but only in the ideological fog that surrounds the concept of race and only for the purpose of a limited integration of some individuals from the African American nation into some aspects of White national life. Today the crisis is past so Harlan is being reasserted.

The contemporary decisions of the Court reviewed here show clearly what Harlan explained, the White nation can remain dominant by sticking with color-blind law. The 14th Amendment says that states may not treat individuals differently, all individuals are equal before the law. No regard, no consideration, will be given to the race or class of the individual. Thus, the Court now says that various government agencies, local and federal, have been used in an unconstitutional "color-conscious" way. These governments have been classifying individuals by race, and presenting statistical evidence as proof of unequal treatment. In so doing they have discriminated against White people. Races do not exist before the law and governments must behave accordingly.

The Civil Rights Acts of 1964 forbid racial discrimination in employment. The truth is that the Civil Rights Act of 1866 and 1871 also forbid discrimination in employment (Edwards 1977:89). As noted, if the law merely forbids discrimination, not much happens. Presidents Lyndon Johnson and Richard Nixon understood that well enough to institute affirmative action. But now the color-blind conservatives say that this must be ended. Discrimination can only be claimed by individuals, case by case, they say. Evidence of discriminatory behavior must be presented and intent to discriminate must be shown.

All this blindness derives from the ideology of the free individual in the marketplace. In the marketplace, individuals are free to buy and sell or do neither. Classes and races do not meet in the marketplace, only individuals. If individuals do wrong in the marketplace, bring them before the court. You can bring a merchant before the court but not the class of merchants, or the system that makes them possible.

Yet the evidence is that, first, African Americans were bought and sold in the marketplace, then held in sharecropping labor by the marketplace, and then in the ghetto by the marketplace. And it should be noted that, although it was the marketplace that did this not the state, the 14th Amendment only says what the state may not do in its treatment of individuals.

What this reveals, of course, is the problem with the constitution. The basic structure of society is made up of the divisions of class, nation, gender, and the contradictions arising therefrom. The constitution knows only an ideal society, Eden, in which such things do not exist. This inverted constitution is indeed a creation of the inverted material world. So, too, are the color-blind conservatives such as Eastland and Bennett, and Judges O'Connor and Thomas. These people stand in a line of ideologists that reaches back to the dawn of inequality in human societies. Like ancient priests, they explain that in the eyes of a great, pure, universal power, all are equal.

The crisis of nationwide ghetto uprisings seems to be in the past. The African American nation exists in a significantly altered, more quiescent form. The USSR is gone. Today the ruling class is saying, "enough," put an end to government involvement in various racial reforms. The Court of today is negating the Court of yesterday and the Democratic party is collapsing into the Republican party on the issue of race.

A "SOUTHERN STRATEGY" FOR THE DEMOCRATIC PARTY

The formation of the Democratic Leadership Council (DLC) was announced in February 1985. The core of the DLC was composed of young, White, southern politicians. It was created to respond to the failure of the Democratic party to win presidential elections and the steady erosion of electoral strength in Congressional elections. The actual goal of the DLC was to move the politics of the Democratic party in the direction of the Republican party, to adopt as its own, many of the positions of the Republicans that were popular with the electorate. As "New Democrats" they would address issues such as welfare reform, a balanced budget, crime, "reinventing government," "individual responsibility," and so forth. These issues all carry a "coded" message to White voters, the Democratic party would no longer be a party in which African Americans had such a strong influence (Hale 1995; Edsall and Edsall 1991). To this end, the DLC had to deal with Jessie Jackson.

In 1984, Jessie Jackson ran for president in the Democratic primaries and won 19 percent of the total votes. He won in four states and the District of Columbia. He got 80 percent of the African American votes that were cast. Jackson had also emerged as the focal point of liberals, the left, and various activist groups within the Democratic party. In the election, Reagan carried 49 states against Mondale while Mondale got 90 percent of the African American vote (Marable 1995). In 1988, Jackson, now head of the Rainbow Coalition, ran again in the primaries and came in second to Dukakis (Marable 1995:59). He got 30 percent of all primary votes, more than any other of the candidates. He won five states in the South and came in second in eight other states.

Jackson was at his peak of electoral popularity in 1988. But conservative Democrats blamed Jackson and his politics for the Dukakis defeat. By 1989, Jackson was under serious pressure from party and Coalition conservatives. At the same time, those on the left wanted him to leave the party and start a new, independent party. Instead, Jackson decided to move to the right. He appointed his own Rainbow Coalition leaders instead of allowing them to be elected. As a result, thousands on the left quit the organization. Manning Marable saw this as a critical turning point in the Movement.[1] As it turned out, Jackson's decision to turn to the right did not help him at all when the conservative DLC took control of the Democratic party (Marable 1995:58).

By 1991 to 1992 the DLC had a budget of more than 2 million dollars. It was mainly funded by 57 corporations and 12 professional or trade associations. These included energy, health care, insurance, pharmaceutical, retail, and tobacco industries (Hale 1995:220).

Bill Clinton, who became chair of the DLC in 1990, was the choice of the organization for president in 1992. With the support of certain "neo-accomodationist" African American leaders, Clinton won the Democratic primaries (Marable 1995:58).

It is said that in June 1992, Clinton "humiliated" Jackson at a national meeting of the Rainbow Coalition. During a speech, Clinton denounced Sister Souljah, a rap singer, who had previously received an award from the Rainbow Coalition for her work with youth (Rueter 1995:23). Sister Soulhjah had said that because White people kill African Americans every day, African Americans should have one day to kill White people. This was Clinton's way of demonstrating the distance between himself and Jessie Jackson. The media, which had been tipped off by Clinton aides, reported the incident widely (Marable 1995:59). This event was analogous to the Willie Horton ad in the 1988 Bush campaign. Even though it was much less racist, presumably, the message was not lost on the White voter. Clinton avoided being photographed with Jackson and kept him at a distance throughout the campaign. Toward the end, Jackson reluctantly endorsed the Clinton campaign (Marable 1995).

African American voters gave their usual support to the Democratic candidate. Marable's analysis is that it was the vast growth of the African American middle class that made it possible to wipe out Jessie Jackson in this way and still get out the African American vote. It was postmovement African American leaders and politicians who mobilized the middle class. This class was much more likely to vote than the lower class of African Americans who made up a significant part of Jessie Jackson's constituency (Marable 1995:68).

In May 1992, south-central Los Angeles erupted following the acquittal of police officers involved in the videotaped, brutal beating of Rodney King, an African American who failed to stop his car when ordered. When the uprising was over, 54 were dead, 2,000 injured, 17,000 arrested, and about 1 billion dollars worth of property destroyed. Although this uprising resembled earlier ones in many ways, this one had a large number of White and Hispanic participants. The event demonstrated that the potential for huge, urban uprisings was still there and that police oppression would trigger it. Both presidential candidates talked "law and order" and kept a low profile on the uprising (Fineman 1992).

Adolph Reed, Jr. (quoted in Rueter 1995) made this astute observation about Clinton's campaign:

> From the first, the Clinton campaign has reminded me of Southern "liberals" under Jim Crow who came to Black voters quitely saying, "I'm really your friend. Of course, I have to call you 'niggers' and appeal to the segregationist vote, but I don't really mean it. I didn't like it, and I'am only doing it to get elected. Afterward I'll take care of you; trust me." (P. 391)

It should be noted that in his electoral victory in 1992, Clinton did not do all that well in the South. He carried only his home state of Arkansas, Vice President Gore's Tennessee, and Louisiana and Georgia.

In his first 2 years in office Clinton appeared entirely too liberal to his critics. He was attacked for his support for gays in the military and for increasing taxes on the very rich. When he nominated Lani Guinier, an African American woman, to be Assistant Attorney General, Guinier was called a "quota queen" by conservative critics because of her writings on African American disfranchisement. Clinton quickly distanced himself from her and dropped all support for her (Guinier 1994). In the fall of 1993 at a meeting of African American church leaders in Memphis, Clinton chastised African Americans in general for a breakdown of values and the family. Like the Sister Souljah incident, this was popular with conservatives. When he mounted a major effort to create a national system of health care, however, conservatives in both parties scuttled the effort leaving Clinton looking ineffective and without direction.

In the 1994 Congressional elections, Republicans trounced the Democrats and captured both houses. Sixty-two percent of White males voted Republican (Fineman 1995). As noted previously, the Republicans made particularly big gains in the South. The House of Representatives, lead by Newt Gingrich, launched what they called a "revolution" to overturn all vestiges of the New Deal. When they tried to attack things such as Medicare, however, public opinion turned decisively against them. Clinton followed a more "centerist" line. He created plans to balance the budget, allocate funds for more police, expand the death penalty, and so forth. He brought in Dick Morris as an adviser. Morris, a Republican consultant, had run Republican Senator Jesse Helms's campaign in 1990 against an African American candidate in North Carolina (Klein 1996).[2] In that campaign, a notorious political advertisement was used suggesting that African American's were taking White jobs because of affirmative action. Although Clinton's popularity increased dramatically, he found himself caught in a dilemma of his own making on the issues of affirmative action and welfare. He wanted to appease the White nation on these issues while not losing the loyalty of the African American nation to the Democratic party. Ultimately, the choice was clear, African Americans have no other place to go with their votes.

In February 1995, President Clinton ordered a review of all federal affirmative action programs. He observed, in that context, that many White males were distressed by declining incomes ("Clinton Opens Conversation" 1995). In June 1995, the Supreme Court announced its *Adarand* decision declaring that government set-asides were unconstitutional. Also in June, Pete Wilson, the Republican governor of California and a presidential contender, announced that he would curtail all state affirmative action programs wherever the law permitted ("Unfair Quotas for Affirmative Action" 1995). In July, at Wilson's urging, the University of California Board of Regents voted to end all affirmative action including admissions, hiring, and contracts ("Affirmative Action Sent Reeling" 1995).

In July 1995, Clinton announced his plans for affirmative action with the slogan, "Mend it, don't end it." He was against quotas, reverse discrimination, preferences for the unqualified, and continuing any programs that could be ended. At the same time, he said that "affirmative action had been good for America" and he supported it (Grady 1995).

In the same month, Republicans Bob Dole and Charles Canady introduced a bill cleverly called the "Equal Opportunity Act of 1996." It would have prohibited the government from giving any kind of preference in employment, contracts, or any program on the basis of race, color, national origin, or gender. Dole, a presidential contender, had once been a strong supporter of affirmative action ("GOP Will Not Try to End Affirmative Action" 1996).

In October 1995, Clinton acquiesced to the Supreme Court's *Adarand* decision. He ordered the Defense Department to suspend the largest affirmative action program in the government, the Pentagon's 1 billion dollar a year set-aside program ("Pentagon Will Suspend Rule" 1995). In March

1996, Clinton suspended all government set-asides for 3 years. In May, he proposed a new set of rules to limit and gradually end preferences in government contracting. To be specific, past discrimination should be demonstrated and programs should be terminated when bias is remedied. Safeguards against minority "front" companies would be expanded. "Socially disadvantaged" businesses headed by nonminorities would be eligible for affirmative action ("Administration Proposes Affirmative Action Limits" 1996).

In July 1996, Bob Dole, the winner of the Republican primaries, withdrew the Dole-Canady "Equal Opportunity Act of 1996" ("GOP Will Not Try to End Affirmative Action" 1996).

Bill Clinton's most striking proposal during his 1992 campaign was that he would "end welfare as we know it." This slogan came out of the DLC analysis of the welfare problem. Politically, the problem was that the Republicans attracted many White votes with their attack on welfare. When White voters hear the word "welfare," they think "Black people." All sides agreed that the welfare system needed to be changed. The DLC developed a line of attack that was essentially the same as the Republican one. The DLC said that welfare had led to a "cycle of dependency," it had destroyed the initiative of individuals to get work. It was the cause of much of teenage pregnancy because young girls and women were deliberately having children to collect welfare. The solution was to end welfare "as we know it." The main difference between the Republican and the Democratic approach to ending welfare was that the Democrats wanted to spend a significant amount of money for such things as education, job training, child care, and so forth (Edsall and Edsall 1991; Hale 1995).

Clinton's bill, calling for such funding, died in Congress early in his administration. The Republican-dominated Congress passed two welfare bills that Clinton vetoed. Then, in August 1995, with the election just 4 months away, the Republicans presented him with a third bill. He signed it.

This bill terminated the federal commitment to the program that had provided assistance to mothers with dependent children for six decades, since the New Deal. It gave block grants of money to the states along with most of the control of welfare programs. Instead of adding money for education and job training, the budget would be cut by about one fifth when it is fully implemented in 2002. There was a 2-year limit on assistance without getting a job and a 5-year lifetime limit. Medicare was continued for recipients. Stricter eligibility standards would exclude many disabled children. Noncitizens would no longer receive benefits and food stamps.

Future immigrants who are not citizens would not receive benefits for their first 5 years in the country. It was estimated that these cuts would save 55 billion dollars over 6 years (Killborn 1996). The Urban Institute noted that the 5-year limit on receiving welfare would hit African Americans the hardest. Roughly equal numbers of White and African Americans receive AFDC, the main welfare program (Passell 1996). Currently, African Americans comprise 49 percent of those on welfare for longer than 5 years, Whites are 25 percent, Hispanics 19 percent, and others are 7 percent (Pear 1996). This raises a question about the "dependency" thesis. Conservatives, Republicans, and Democrats argue that poverty is not the cause of welfare but welfare is the cause of poverty. Because African Americans and Whites are subjected to the same causal factor, welfare, why is it that African Americans have double the dependency of Whites? Perhaps racial oppression explains the difference. Perhaps racial and class oppression explain why welfare is simply the best choice available for survival for all those at the bottom of society. At any rate, African Americans will indeed be hard hit by this bill. The inner-city is especially lacking in jobs and this bill provides nothing to create the jobs that it demands the poor must get. Senator Patrick Moynihan called it "the most brutal act of social policy since Reconstruction" (Killborn and Verhovek 1996).

NOTES

1. *The Movement* was a term that included the civil rights movement, the Black Power Movement and other Black nationalist movements, the anti-Vietnam War Movement, the New Left, the Native American Movement, Chicano Movement, Women's Movement, and so forth.

2. Dick Morris's relationship with President Clinton went back to 1977 and Clinton's election as governor of Arkansas. He assisted Clinton in 1982 in regaining the office of governor. Morris won out over more liberal advisers when Clinton signed the Welfare Reform Act in 1996. Morris was said to have remarked that this would lock up the reelection of Clinton (Fineman and Turque 1996:25). Morris was also a strong advocate of the president pushing "values" such as opposition to young people smoking cigarettes, the V-chip in television sets, uniforms for children in public schools, and so forth. Morris said that he wanted Clinton to run more as "pope than president" and act as a moral guide for teenagers. Morris resigned in early September 1996 after it was learned that he had regularly employed the services of a prostitute in the expensive hotel room in Washington provided for him by the Democratic National Committee (Berke 1996).

REFERENCES

Adarand v. Pena, 115 S. Ct. 2097 (1995).

"Administration Proposes Affirmative Action Limits." 1996. *Virginian-Pilot,* May 23, p. A4.

"Affirmative Action Sent Reeling." 1995. *Virginian-Pilot,* July 21, pp. A1 & A9.

Berke, Richard L. 1996. "Clinton Aide Dick Morris Quits Over Tie to Call Girl." *New York Times,* August 30.

Blackwell, James. 1991. *The Black Community.* New York: HarperCollins.

Bundy, McGeorge. 1977. "The Issue Before the Court: Who Gets Ahead in America." *Atlantic Monthly,* November, pp. 44-45.

Carmines, Edward and James A. Stimson. 1989. *Issue Evolution: Race and the Transformation of American Politics.* Princeton, NJ: Princeton University Press.

City of Richmond v. Croson, 109 S. Ct. at 754-57 (Marshall, J. dissenting, 1989).

"Clinton Opens 'Conversation' on Affirmative Action Programs." 1995. *Virginian-Pilot,* July 9.

Eastland, Terry. 1996. *Ending Affirmative Action: The Case for Affirmative Action.* New York: Basic Books.

Eastland, Terry and William J. Bennett. 1979. *Counting by Race.* New York: Basic Books.

Edsall, Thomas B. and Mary D. Edsall. 1991. *Chain Reaction: The Impact of Race, Rights, and Taxes on American Politics.* New York: W. W. Norton.

Edwards, Harry T. 1977. "Racial Discrimination in Employment: What Price Equality?" Pp. 71-144 in *Civil Liberties and Civil Rights,* edited by V. Stone. Urbana: University of Illinois Press.

Fineman, Howard. 1992. "Leadership? Don't Ask Us." *Newsweek* May 11, p. 42.

Fineman, Howard. 1995. "Race and Rage." *Newsweek,* April 3.

Fineman, Howard and Bill Turque. 1996. "How He Got His Groove." *Newsweek,* September 2, pp. 21-25.

Fullilove v. Klutznick, 448 U.S. 448 (1980).

Gamson, William and Andre Modigliani. 1987. "The Changing Culture of Affirmative Action." *Research in Political Sociology* 3:137-77.

Glazer, Nathan. 1975. *Affirmative Discrimination: Ethnic Inequality and Public Policy.* Cambridge, MA: Harvard University Press.

"GOP Will Not Try to End Affirmative Action This Year." 1996. *Virginian-Pilot,* July 15, A2.

Grady, Sandy. 1995. "Clinton Stood His Ground." *Philadelphia Daily News,* July 7.

Guinier, Lani. 1994. *The Tyranny of the Majority.* New York: Free Press.

Hacker, Andrew. 1995. *Two Nations.* New York: Ballentine.

Hale, Jon F. 1995. "The Making of the New Democrats." *Political Science Quarterly* 110:2.

Harris, Louis. 1996. "The Future of Affirmative Action." Pp. 323-340 in *The Affirmative Action Debate,* edited by G. E. Curry. Reading, MA: Addison-Wesley.

Hofstader, Richard and Beatrice K. Hofstader. 1982. *Great Issues in American History.* New York: Vintage.

Herrnstein, Richard and Charles Murray. 1994. *The Bell Curve: Intelligence and Class Structure in American Life.* New York: Free Press.

Jensen, Arthur. 1973. *Educability and Group Differences.* New York: Harper and Row.

Kelly, Michael. 1995. "Segregation Anxiety." *The New Yorker,* November, pp. 43-54.

Kerbo, Harold R. 1991. *Social Stratification and Inequality.* New York: McGraw-Hill.

Killborn, Peter. 1996. "With Welfare Overhaul Now Law, States Grapple With Consequences." *New York Times,* July 23.

Killborn, Peter T. and Sam Howe Verhovek. 1996. "The Clinton Record (Part 2)." *New York Times,* August 2.

Klein, Joe. 1996. "How Clinton Could Screw Up." *Newsweek,* February 26, p. 30.

Lenski, Gerhard. 1996. *Power and Privilege.* New York: McGraw-Hill.

Lind, Michael. 1996. *The Next American Nation.* New York: Free Press.

Lively, Donald E. 1992. *The Constitution and Race.* New York: Praeger.

Lublin, David. 1995. "Race, Representation, and Redistricting." Pp. 111-128 in *Classifying by Race,* edited by Paul E. Peterson. Princeton, NJ: Princeton University Press.

Marable, Manning. 1995. *Beyond Black and White: Transforming African American Politics.* New York: Verso.

Metro Broadcasting v. Federal Communications Commission, 110 S. Ct. 2997 (1990).

"On Tape, Texaco Officials Talk of Destroying Files in Lawsuit." 1996. *Virginian-Pilot,* November 4, p. A2.

"Pentagon Will Suspend Rule That Helped Minority Businesses." 1995. *Virginian-Pilot,* October 22, p. A7.

Passell, Peter. 1996. "Economic Scene: Welfare to Workforce—But Will It Work." *New York Times,* August 8.

Pear, Robert. 1996. "Welfare Issues: Poor Likely to Bear Burden of Entitlement Cuts." *New York Times,* July 25.

Pincus, Fred L. 1994. "Toward a Marxist View of Affirmative Action." Presented at the annual meeting of the American Sociological Association, August 6, Los Angeles, CA.

Plessy v. Ferguson, 163 U.S. 537 (1896).

Polenberg, Richard. 1983. *One Nation Divisible.* New York: Penguin.

Regents of the University of California v. Bakke, 438 U.S. 265 (1978).

Rueter, Theodore. 1995. "The Politics of Race." Pp. 5-26 in *The Politics of Race,* edited by Theodore Rueter. New York: M. E. Sharpe.

Shaw v. Reno. 1993. *United States Law Week,* 4818-34.

Swain, Carol. 1995. "Strategies for Increasing Black Representation in Congress." Pp. 212-225 in *The Politics of Race,* edited by T. Rueter. New York: M. E. Sharpe.

"Texas Districts Redrawn: New Elections Ordered." 1996. *Associated Press,* August 7.

Thronburgh v. Gingles, 478 U.S. 30 (1986).

" 'Unfair' Quotas for Affirmative Action Faces an Ax in California." 1995. *Virginian-Pilot,* June 1.

"Washington Washes Its Hands." 1996. *Newsweek,* August 12.

Wicker, Tom. 1996. *Racial Integration in America: Tragic Failure.* New York: William Morrow.

Willhelm, Sidney. 1976. "Equality: America's Racist Ideology." Pp. 136-57 in *The Death of White Society,* edited by J. Ladner. New York: Vintage.

8

COLOR BLINDNESS:
ILLUSIONS AND CONSEQUENCES

What is the state of "race" relations after 35 years of "color-blind" integration? Despite significant changes, the African American nation still exists, it is still separate in many dimensions, and it is still oppressed. There is still a distinct African American economic structure that is still the inverse of that of the White nation. This material inversion has produced and is sustained by color blindness, the new White nationalist ideology that hides and denies the existence of the African American nation. The difference between liberal and conservative color-blind ideology can be delineated by examining them both in regard to the critical issue of affirmative action—once we clarify what we mean by "racism" and what we do not mean by it.

Integration, repression, and color-blind ideology have killed The Movement—along with the failure of that movement to solve the riddle of "race." The Movement is dead, yet no one thinks the "race" problem is solved. Violence and nationalist eruptions convince some that a "race war" is eminent. The nationalist division of working people still does today what it did in the colonial period: It secures ruling class control of economic and political relations. Today, this division, along with the end of the Cold War, has produced a new era that threatens the income, working conditions, and job security of all who work for a living.

THE AFRICAN AMERICAN NATION TODAY

Certain liberal illusions about the future of "race relations" can no longer be sustained. African Americans are not going to be dispersed among the White population. They are not an "ethnic group" that will be assimilated. They are not a "race" that can be made White by the pretense that people can be color-blind. They are an oppressed nation. They live in North America in the United States, that is their territory. They live, scattered across that territory, in highly concentrated, nearly homogeneous enclaves and within those enclaves are ghettos, which are characterized by profound poverty.

Territory

If we had a projector that could show the racial and ethnic distribution of the population of the United States with a series of overlays, the distinctive situation of the African American nation would be apparent. If we showed the White nation first; then put on an overlay showing the Asian, Hispanic, and other groups; and then the African American population; what we would see first is that the Asian, Hispanic, and other groups are not nearly as isolated from the White population as the African American. If we could do the same thing going back in time, we would see that European ethnic groups never lived in the kind of isolation that African Americans continue to experience today. Thus, African Americans are unique in their isolation from the White population. We would also see that this isolation increased dramatically in major American cities as a result of the Northern migration and the subsequent White flight from neighborhoods and cities (Massey and Denton 1993).

It was a liberal illusion that if African Americans became more prosperous, they would be accepted into White communities. The fact is that African Americans are isolated at all levels of income. And the minority of African Americans who live in suburbs are also isolated (Massey and Denton 1993).

In 1990, 74 percent of Whites lived in suburban areas whereas the majority of African Americans and Hispanics live in urban areas (Wilson 1994:2). The 1990 census showed that African Americans are in the majority in 14 American cities with a population over 100,000. They range from 51.3 percent of the population to 59.2 percent in 8 cities. In 4 cities they range from 61.9 percent to 67.1 percent of the population. They are

76 percent of the population in Detroit, Michigan, and 80 percent in Gary, Indiana (Marger 1994:263).

Massey and Denton (1993) developed a measure of "hypersegregation" that uses five dimensions of residential segregation. It defines the ghetto. They analyzed 30 metropolitan areas (cities and suburbs) and identified 16 that contained the largest ghettos. Altogether these 16 areas contained 35 percent of the total African American population in the United States. Three of the 16 were in the South. The people living in these areas, which are in the urban core, have little or no contact with anyone other than African Americans (Massey and Denton 1993:77-8).

The Fair Housing Law was passed by Congress in 1968 and revised in 1988. The focus of that law, and the focus of local laws as well, on individual violations means that there is no legal force that can cope with the forces that produce the residential isolation of African Americans. Those forces consist of things such as banks, insurance companies, zoning practices, real estate offices, urban renewal, public housing placement, and so forth (Marger 1994:272-73). In other words, these elements operating in the base of society produce law in such a way that it cannot significantly influence the isolation of the African American nation from the White nation in the United States. Social scientists can predict with great accuracy the rate of White flight in relation to the percentage of African Americans present in a neighborhood—it starts below 10 percent African American (Hacker 1995:42). Taueber and Taueber (cited in Massey and Denton 1993:247) studied the process in six northern cities. They described stages with the following terms: all white, invasion, succession, consolidation, or all black. They found that 90 percent of all neighborhoods inhabited by African Americans in 1960 were either all African American or moving in that direction in 1970.

With so much attention given to urban developments, rural African Americans are often overlooked. It is estimated that there are 2,000,000 impoverished African Americans in rural areas, mainly concentrated in the South (Blackwell 1991:91).

Kuame Ture (Stokely Carmichael), the African American nationalist, was once accused of being a "separatist." His reply was simply, "We *are* separate."[1] After a quarter century of integration, it would take an illusionist to look at the available data and say that these two nations are not separate or to insist that something is going to change this in the foreseeable future. In short, the African American nation lives in the United States mainly in scattered, separate territories, surrounded by mainly separate White territories.

Politics

Although most African American political effort has taken place within mainstream parties, they have also formed their own political parties at either the state or national level for over 100 years (Blackwell 1991:368). Early organizations were the National Independent Political League (1912), the National Labor Congress (1924), and the National Negro Congress (1936). Such efforts in the 1960s at the local level included the Mississippi Freedom Democratic Party and the Black Panther Party in Lowndes county, Alabama. In recent times, at the national level, there has been the Afro-American Party (1960), the Freedom Now Party (1964), the Peace and Freedom Party (1968). The National Black Independent Political Party was founded in 1980. This party was one of more than 10 nationalist organizations that was represented at a national conference held in New York in 1981. The conference agreed on the following resolutions: African Americans were an oppressed nation, had the right of self-determination, and should receive reparations from the United States (Ola 1981). Blackwell (1991:369) noted that these efforts have typically been short lived.

There are a great many national African American political organizations and coalitions today. To name a few, these include the Black United Front, the Leadership Conference on Civil Rights, Black Leadership Forum, NAACP, Operation PUSH, Southern Christian Leadership Conference, and the National Council of Negro Women (Blackwell 1991:368). African Americans in the Congress have also formed their own Black Caucus. These race-conscious organizations exist in a dialectical relationship with official government bodies dominated by the White nation.

Between 1970 and 1989, the number of African American elected officials had increased by almost 500 percent. They are 1.4 percent of all elected officials in the United States (Blackwell 1991:356). Most of these officials are elected at the local level. Ten large cities with African American majorities have elected African American mayors. It has been noted, however, that it can be a hollow victory to win election to office in a bankrupt city where White flight to the suburbs has undercut the tax base. Furthermore, mayors have power that is more symbolic than real because business people tend to dictate the actual life of a city (Marger 1994). Although it is true that 22 cities of various sizes with a minority of African Americans have elected African American mayors (Hacker 1995:217), the general pattern is that African American electoral success depends on having an African American majority. Success in state elections, for example, is largely dependent on have concentrated voting districts. Thus, most of the elected African American state officials are found in the South. As noted in the previous chapter, election to Congress is highly dependent on the existence of African American-majority districts.

The notion that people "who happen to be Black" will be randomly elected to office in a color-blind fashion is no longer believable. Such elections accomplish very little anyway if one recognizes that the African American nation, as such, deserves political representation. American-style democracy with the "winner-take-all" electoral college system operates against all kinds of minority blocks. For example, if African Americans formed their own party, not only would they lose, but so would the Democratic party. Even if there was proportional representation, that would still leave African Americans as a small minority in elected bodies (see Guinier 1994). There seems to be no possibility that African Americans will be able to fundamentally alter their condition through their own efforts in the existing political system. In the light of recent Supreme Court "color-blind" decisions against African American-majority voting districts, the trend is clearly in the direction of diminished representation at the national level and probably at the state level as well.

Economy

Although there is a separate African American economy, non-African Americans dominate business within the African American nation (Blackwell 1991:303). About one half of all African American-owned businesses provide personal services such as restaurants, bars, food stores, car dealerships, service stations, barber shops, and so forth (Blackwell 1991:303). Eighty-five percent of African American businesses have no paid employees (Hacker 1995:113). Of the 100 largest companies, only 10 have as many as 1,000 employees. The 25 largest African American owned banks only employ a total of 1,740 people (Hacker 1995:113). Along with African American-owned banks, there are savings and loan associations, life insurance companies, radio and TV stations, and franchises—all of which tend to serve an exclusively African American clientele. African American enterprises have a high failure rate due to undercapitalization. They have extremely high insurance rates due to the high probability of robbery. They also have inordinate losses resulting from employee theft, embezzlement, pilferage, and fraud (Blackwell 1991:326).

There is a "huge" underground economy involving organized crime, gambling, drugs, stolen property, prostitution, and so forth (Blackwell 1991:326).

Only part of the flood of African American migrants to American cities was absorbed by the larger capitalist economy. African American unemployment, for example, is generally twice the level of White unemployment regardless of the state of the economy. African Americans who finish college still have double the unemployment of Whites (Hacker 1995:109.). The government, therefore, has had to sustain a significant part of the African American population with welfare and with expanded government employment.

About 15.5 percent of all African American households receive AFDC welfare and 26 percent receive food stamps. That compares to 2 percent of White households on AFDC and 4.6 percent receiving food stamps (Edsall and Edsall 1991:162).

The household that has only one wage earner is especially vulnerable to poverty. Of all White families, 59 percent have two or more wage earners whereas only 47 percent of African American have two or more (12 percent less). About 7.2 percent of all White families live in poverty and, of those families in poverty, 24.2 percent are headed by females. Among African Americans, 31 percent of families live in poverty and 50 percent are headed by females. In 1960, only 11.5 percent of African American households headed by women had never married. By 1993, the figure was 55.4 percent (Hacker 1995:80). Whereas today 10 percent of all White women in their 40s have never married, 25 percent of African American women have never married. The proportion of female-headed African American families today is much higher than it was prior to the post-World War II urban migration (Macionis 1997:469).

African American women make up 51 percent of total African American employment, but in professional, managerial, and technical employment they make up 65 percent, 52 percent, and 57 percent, respectively, of total African American employment in those fields (Hacker 1995:108). African American women show some income gain with every level of educational improvement and their earnings are almost on a par with White women when they have college and advanced degrees. About twice as many African American women as men are completing college degrees. About 56 percent of these women are married compared to 71 percent of White women. By the 1980s, African American men had closed the gap between their earnings and those of White men to about 75 percent but the gap got larger again in the 1990s, declining to 72 percent (Hacker 1995:108). African American men remain well below White men in income at all levels of education (Hacker 1995:101).

Half of all African Americans holding professional and managerial-level jobs are employed by local, state, or federal government agencies (Edsall and Edsall 1991:18). African Americans make up 20 percent of the armed services and they hold one fifth of the jobs in the postal service (Hacker 1995:121). Aided by affirmative action, by 1980, African Americans and other minorities held 23 percent of all federal jobs (Blackwell 1991:87). It can be seen, then, that cutbacks in government employment, in the military, and in welfare, along with privatization of mail delivery, pose grave threats to the progress that has been made by African Americans in employment.

Class Structure

Blackwell's (1991) analysis of the class structure of African America suggests that it resembles the class structure of White America but the elements are in very different proportions. Hacker (1995) showed the income distribution for African Americans and Whites for the years 1970 and 1992 (Figure 8.1).

A striking thing about these distributions is that they are the inverse of each other in both time periods. This represents rather well the material, national contradiction in the base of society that gives rise to ideological inversions such as the notion that White people, generally, are the victims of reverse discrimination. In 1970, the African American distribution is a pyramid whereas the White distribution is an inverted pyramid. In 1992, the African American distribution had a slightly upward tapering column arising from a large base. The White distribution had a slightly tapering column descending from a large top.

This suggests that the comparative richness of the income of the White nation is linked to the poverty of the African American nation and that this link persists even when there are changes in the income distribution of both nations.

A trend toward greater income inequality can be seen in the income distribution of both nations between these two time periods. Hacker (1995) has shown that African Americans have gained much greater access to some occupations but not where the rewards are the greatest. Still, Figure 8.1 clearly shows the movement of a significant proportion of African Americans into higher income levels.

About 15 percent of African American families are affluent with incomes over $50,000. These families are more likely to depend on two wage earners than comparable White families, and their incomes are also more

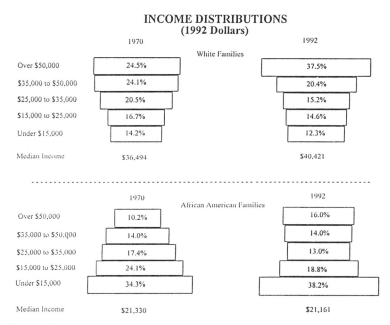

INCOME DISTRIBUTIONS
(1992 Dollars)

1970   1992

White Families

	1970	1992
Over $50,000	24.5%	37.5%
$35,000 to $50,000	24.1%	20.4%
$25,000 to $35,000	20.5%	15.2%
$15,000 to $25,000	16.7%	14.6%
Under $15,000	14.2%	12.3%
Median Income	$36,494	$40,421

African American Families

	1970	1992
Over $50,000	10.2%	16.0%
$35,000 to $50,000	14.0%	14.0%
$25,000 to $35,000	17.4%	13.0%
$15,000 to $25,000	24.1%	18.8%
Under $15,000	34.3%	38.2%
Median Income	$21,330	$21,161

Figure 8.1.
SOURCE: Reprinted with the permission of Scribner, a Division of Simon & Schuster from *Two Nations: Black and White Separate, Hostile, Unequal* by Andrew Hacker. Copyright © by Andrew Hacker.

likely to come from salaries than from investments. On average, African American families earned 65 percent of what White families earned in the 1980s, but that had fallen to 54 percent by 1992 (Macionis 1995:271).

To realize such growth in the middle class and upper class required the civil rights and Black Power struggle, ghetto uprisings, boycotts, lawsuits, laws, executive orders, affirmative action, and so forth. Clearly, significant occupation integration has taken place but without a corresponding process of assimilation. And as Feagan and Sikes (1994) have reported, many middle-class African Americans experience discrimination on the job as well as in most other aspects of their lives.

The African American Church and University

The church is one of the most important forms of social organization in the African American community and it is almost a completely separate institution. Baptists are the largest denomination followed by Methodists, Muslims, and many smaller denominations. The church plays a vital role in combating national oppression with leadership, charity, teaching, business activities, and political activism (Blackwell 1991). As noted earlier, Franklin Frazier (1963) called the African American church the nation within a nation. It is for this reason that White nationalists have burned and bombed African American church buildings for so long. There was a sudden upsurge in burnings in 1996, a presidential election year that featured powerful attacks on affirmative action and the like. About 100 churches were burned across the South ("Wave of Church Burnings" 1996).

Four out of five African American college students attend integrated colleges or universities. One in five attend one of the 96 colleges or universities that are "historically Black" (Hacker 1995). African American students on integrated campuses often associate with each other rather than with White students. In recent years there have been numerous, blatantly racist incidents across the country on integrated campuses (Jones 1991).

Culture, Beliefs, and Ideology

Cultural nationalism, as opposed to revolutionary nationalism, makes internal cultural practices the focus of change rather than external political change. Ron Karenga (Allen 1970:165-69) founded US following the Watts riots. He came to be recognized as one of the chief proponents of cultural nationalism in the 1960s. Afrocentricity is the name given to the movement that promotes African heritage and culture. Great attention is given to African music, fashion, hair styles, life styles, food, art, literature, history, and religion. Critics have noted that cultural nationalism often seems to turn into a form of Black capitalism.

Massey and Denton (1993:165) have noted how the inner-city ghetto continues to produce a "Black English" dialect. Early in 1997, a furious controversy erupted when the Oakland School Board adopted a resolution saying that "Ebonics" was a language and needed to be taken into account in teaching. Critics, including NAACP President Kweisi Mfume and Secretary of Education Richard Riley, insisted it was not a language and that only "Standard English" should be permitted in the schools ("Oakland to Change" 1997). "Standard English" is White English, the language of the White nation. An adage exists that says that a language is a dialect with an army (Leland and Joseph 1997). There is research that shows that African American students do better in school when they are in programs that recognize the bilingual nature of their situation. Some major school systems already have such programs operating (see Gadsden and Wagner 1995).

Needless to say, the African American nation constantly creates its own styles of music, dance, art, poetry, writing, humor, speech, clothing, customs, and so forth. African American television channels, radio stations, magazines, and newspapers provide communication throughout the nation. "Lift Ev'ry Voice and Sing," written in 1900, is considered to be the national anthem of the African American nation.

It is well documented that African Americans have some beliefs that are very different from White Americans. O. J. Simpson, a former professional football player and African American, was acquitted of murdering his White ex-wife in October 1995. There was extensive live coverage of the trial on television for months prior to the verdict. A *Newsweek* poll showed that 85 percent of African Americans agreed with the verdict while 32 percent of Whites agreed with it (Whitaker 1995). A national poll taken in 1994 showed that 26 percent of African Americans, compared to 51 percent of Whites, agreed with the statement, "We've gone too far in pushing equal rights in this country." In the same poll, 73 percent of African Americans, compared to 43 percent of Whites, agreed that, "In the past few years there hasn't been much improvement in the position of Blacks" ("Racial Overtones Color GOP Reforms, Some Say" 1995). A national poll taken in 1993 found that 51 percent of African Americans agreed that "the United States is moving toward two separate and unequal societies—one Black, one White." Only a third of Whites agreed with the statement. When asked if African Americans have as good a chance as Whites to get jobs for which they are qualified, twice as many Whites as African Americans said yes (Marable 1995:146).

The author conducted a campus study in 1992 that included a question on color-blind ideology (see the appendix). Students at a mid-Atlantic university were asked to agree or disagree with the statement, "I'm color-blind when it comes to race." The results are seen in Figure 8.2.

The majority of African American students responded in the negative. Sixty percent indicated that they were not color-blind when it came to race. Inversely, 77 percent of White students said that they were color-blind when it came to race. In a follow-up study in 1996, students were asked to explain what they meant if they said they were color-blind. The typical answer from White and African American students was that being color-blind meant that they did not discriminate and were not prejudiced or that race means nothing to them. The majority of African Americans who said that they were not color-blind said things like it was impossible to be African American and be color-blind in America. When in-depth discus-

"I am color-blind when it comes to race"

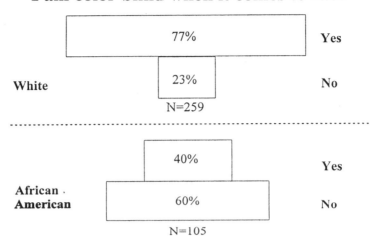

Figure 8.2.

sions were held with African American students about this question, some said that they found the notion of color blindness to be offensive. In other words, the pretense that they do not exist as African Americans was insulting.

To say that you do not discriminate and are not prejudiced is one thing, to say that you do not do this because you are "color-blind" is something else. But White people can no more be expected to know this than they could have been expected to reject evolutionary racist thought when it was the dominant ideology. Unlike Supreme Court Justice Harlan, most of these students probably did not know that "color blindness" was a term loaded with tricky ideological meaning.

The author's study was limited to one university and the findings cannot be generalized to the whole country. Very little research has been done on color blindness but two studies have produced compatible findings. Ruth Frankenberg (1993:14) characterized color blindness as "color evasiveness and power evasiveness." She observed that White people do not see themselves as belonging to a White race. Rather, they see themselves as

"American" or "normal." She described one person who saw White culture as "no culture," "Whiteness as nothingness" (Frankenberg 1993:122). Race privilege, she said, is lived but not seen. Similarly, a study of students at Berkeley in 1990 found that some White students felt estranged or bewildered because they had no organizations to belong to that were comparable to the race-based and ethnic-based organizations on campus (Diversity Project 1995).

National Oppression

The incarceration of African Americans today is extraordinary. There is a great fear in the White nation of the African American criminal and it is not without some foundation. The census bureau annual survey of crime victimization shows that African Americans commit 55 percent of all murders, 33 percent of all rapes, and 71 percent of all robberies. For the first two, murder and rape, it is very rare that a White person is the victim of an attack by an African American. But 38 percent of all robberies involved an African American assailant and a White victim (Hacker 1995:191).

The criminal justice system has never provided significant protection from, nor deterrence to, violent crimes. In 1992, 3.3 million reported violent crimes led to only 100,000 convictions (Rosenthal 1996). In other words, a person who commits a violent crime has about 3.3 chances in 100 of going to prison—assuming that all the people who are in prison are the ones who committed the crimes. The United States has one of the highest crime rates in the world. All this adds up to a widespread fear of crime, which politicians have been quick to exploit, with a racial twist.

The incarcerated population in the United States more than doubled between 1985 and 1995 ("Tougher Laws Send Prisons 1996). States now spend an average of 6 percent of their budget on jails, up from under 2 percent in 1980. In states such as Virginia and California, this has been done at the expense of education, especially higher education. California once provided virtually free higher education in one of the best university systems in the country. Today it has quadrupled the fees that students must pay. In 1980, it spent six times as much on higher education as on jails, now it spends more on jails (Lewis 1996). For-profit, privately owned prisons hold 5 percent of the prison population and the top five corporations in this expanding business are considered a "strong buy" by investment counselors (Bryson 1996:28-35).

In 1993, African Americans made up 45 percent of the jail and prison population (Hacker 1995:195). In 1995, one in three African Americans between the ages of 18 and 27 were either in jail, or on probation or parole ("Study: 1 in 3 Young Black Men" 1995).

Drug offenses account for a significant part of the increase in the jail and prison population. In 1980, drug offenders were 8 percent of the jail population. That grew to 25 percent in 1995. Drug offenders were 25 percent of the federal prison population in 1980 but grew to 60 percent in 1995 ("Prisons Nationwide" 1995). Although African Americans were 24 percent of all those arrested for drugs, they were 74 percent of all prisoners serving time on drug charges ("Study: 1 in 3 Young Black Men" 1995).

In addition to greatly expanding the prison population, it has become quite common to "get tough" on prisoners. "Boot camps" are now widespread. In these programs prisoners agree to submit to demeaning, brutal, and authoritarian treatment in hopes of early release. In 1996, Alabama's prison commissioner attracted national attention when he revived the old practice of putting male prisoners in chain gangs. Later, he was fired and the chain gangs terminated when he said he would do the same for female prisoners ("Warden Fired" 1996). In Phoenix, Arizona, however, the sheriff has instituted female chain gangs ("Sheriff Puts First" 1996). The new state prison commissioner in Virginia is known for his harsh, "conservative" approach to inmate treatment. He has barred reporters from the prisons. The Department of Corrections says that it is under no obligation to inform the public of assaults, deaths, escapes, riots, or anything else. Similar policies exist in Illinois, California, and Rhode Island (LaFay 1996).

The "war on drugs" has hit the African American nation so hard that there is a strong suspicion that drug prosecution is a conspiracy. An African American federal district judge in Virginia objected when he learned that prosecutors had granted immunity to White defendants but not to African Americans. When the prosecutors refused to provide the court with information relating to their choice of who to prosecute, the judge threw out the case (Jackson 1995). An African American couple filed suit against Maryland state police who stopped them on the highway and searched them for drugs. Police records showed that 75 percent of the people stopped for this purpose were African American ("75 Percent of Maryland Drug Patrol's" 1996). In Philadelphia, 60 criminal cases were overturned after police officers confessed to planting drugs, falsifying reports, and rigging confessions from poor African Americans. Over 1,400 additional cases were under review ("Philadelphia Police Scandal" 1995). In October 1995,

Congress refused to lower the 5-year mandatory sentence for possession of five or more grams of crack cocaine. Possession of powdered cocaine, generally used by more affluent Whites, carries a much lighter penalty. The decision by Congress set off riots in five federal prisons resulting in 26 people injured and millions of dollars of damage ("Study: 1 in 3 Young Black Men" 1995). African American suspicions were exacerbated by the recent court testimony of a Nicaraguan "contra." He testified that he was part of a group who introduced and sold cocaine in the 1980s to African American gangs in Los Angeles to raise money for CIA operations against the Nicaraguan socialist government ("California Senator" 1996).

Paul Butler, an African American academic and former prosecutor, has pointed out that some African American juries are engaging in jury nullification when African American defendants are brought up on drug charges and other nonviolent charges. In other words, they refuse to convict regardless of the evidence and the law (Butler 1995). Butler has defended the practice saying that the law discriminates. In fact, by tradition, the law allows juries to engage in nullification as a form of protest. Of course, White juries have refused to convict Whites for racist actions on many occasions.

The interesting thing in this African American jury nullification is that the jurors obviously "see" the existence of their race and its special circumstances, whether the law does or not. They refuse to see African American defendants as just individuals. There is a great potential in this for outraged White nationalist reaction as was seen in the case of the O. J. Simpson acquittal. The key issue here is not just that the law discriminates (in indirect ways such as crack vs. powdered cocaine) but that the law is blind to the existence of the African American nation and refuses to take into account the special conditions of its members.

The research of Feagin and Sikes (1994) makes it clear that middle-class African Americans experience racism in virtually all aspects of their lives where they are in contact with White Americans. Lois Benjamin (1991), in *The Black Elite,* has documented the painful experiences of highly successful and wealthy African Americans. Similarly, Ellis Cose (1993) in *The Rage of a Privileged Class,* and bell hooks (1995) in *Killing Rage* show the conflict and personal turmoil that occurs when African Americans try to make it in White capitalist America. One thing that all these books say is that the upward mobility-integration approach has not solved the race problem even when African American individuals have achieved money and position. These books also say the obvious, in a multitude of ways:

White people are acutely color conscious, not color-blind. Nothing reveals this better than attitudes toward affirmative action.

WHO ARE THE COLOR-BLIND?

Carl Rowan, the African American journalist, has looked at the church burnings, racist militia groups, right-wing talk shows, and so forth and predicts that we are headed toward a "race war" (Rowan 1996). He says that

> One of the most inflammatory confrontations in the coming race war has been building up for years, and on many battlefields. Americans are brandishing hand grenades over "affirmative action." (P. 102)

A considerable body of empirical research has tried to test the idea that White opposition to affirmative action is racist. This is an important question, but the research has been plagued with a number of conceptual problems.

First, the tendency has been to see attitudes such as prejudice as the primary cause of race problems. As Wellman (1993:39) put it, "The racial organization of society is thus seen as a consequence of, rather than a cause of people's racial beliefs." Prejudice is a micro-level, social psychological phenomenon, a learned set of beliefs, or it is a psychological phenomenon arising from the personality of the individual. A micro-level phenomenon such as prejudice is an ahistorical concept but it can be incorporated into a historic framework. In such a framework, prejudice and racist ideology can be explained in terms of the structure of inequality in the base of society, which gives rise to both of them. In other words, the racial relations of production in the base of society produce both ideology and prejudice. But conceptual clarification is needed before attempting to look at ideology and prejudice at the micro level.

Racist is a concept that is very confused in both the professional and the popular mind. The term came into widespread use in the social sciences in the 1960s. Simpson and Yinger (1972:721), who expressed their dislike for the term, defined it as "a complex of discriminations and prejudices directed against an alleged inferior race." The long-standing theory was that prejudice was the cause of discrimination. But an "ism" can refer to either beliefs, or practices, or both as is the case with the definition of racism given here. The problem is that discrimination is no longer distinguished from its presumed cause, prejudice. Racism became both the cause and the effect. It was both the phenomenon in question, and the cause of it. This created a major problem (circular reasoning) for the research on "symbolic racism," which first tried to argue that opposition to affirmative action was racist. Some researchers said that those who rejected affirmative action were racists even if they had rejected evolutionary racist ideology. (A review of that research can be found in the Appendix.) This reflected the way the term racist had been transformed to mean not just biological determinists, but all those who appeared to be acting against the interests of African Americans. In addition, researchers did not clearly distinguish ideology from prejudice in either theory or measurement. They typically treated both concepts as "beliefs" that arise in the general population that "rationalize" inequality. Marx, of course, viewed ideology as the product of elite intellectuals who picked up the biased notions of the ruling class and turned them into theories. Both the biases of the ruling class and the theories of their intellectuals ultimately arise from the material structure of society and its contradictions.

There is an additional problem with the term racist that was previously discussed. It does not distinguish between the racism of the oppressor and the oppressed. People speak of "Black racism" as if the African American antagonism against Whites is the equivalent of White antagonism against African Americans. As Fanon (1963) argued, the antagonism emanating from an oppressed people is not the same as the antagonism of the oppressor. This is the same error that occurs in bourgeois law—treating as equals, individuals from classes or races that are not equal. That there is no way to make this distinction, that there is only the term racist, is an ideological phenomenon.

The name given to the subject of inquiry is critical. The name should express the essence of the subject. It made all the difference, for example, when Marx called capitalism, capitalism and analyzed it as such. When capitalism is called "industrial society," nearly everything that follows is different. Evolutionary racist ideologists erroneously called African Americans a race. Even though the era of evolutionary racist ideology is past, modern-day social scientists and others continue to use the same term. They say they mean race as a social thing rather than a biological thing. The question is, however, what would they have called African Americans if they had not continued to use the term originally employed by racist ideologists? What is the social thing called race? (We recall that only certain Marxists persisted in using the term "nation" when most of the rest of the capitalist world adopted "race" with its biological determinist meaning.)

In truth, modern social scientists do recognize a biological factor as critical, the inheritance by African Americans of those physical characteristics that now are called "Black." Inherited physical appearance plays an important role in race because it identifies the members of the African American nation. Racist oppression could not occur without identification, but is identification the essence of the phenomenon? Under Fascist conquest, Jews were made to wear yellow stars so they could be racially identified. The stars may have facilitated the oppression of Jews but obviously they were not the essence of it. The term race keeps the focus on the biological factor that produces identification, or "visibility." This leads directly to the color-blind, assimilation solution to the race problem. If racists defined race into existence, the solution is to define it out of existence. (This is pure idealism.) African American individuals will be liberated from their race and dissolved into the White nation. Underneath this is the old wish to make African Americans disappear, a wish that is genocidal in spirit. "Nation," of course, does not fit into this scheme at all, it affirms identity and necessarily implies a political and collective solution. Race is no more the essence of the African American situation than religion is the essence of the Irish situation. African American people are largely a mixed-race people with African ancestry as their primary identification. The existence of African American people as an oppressed nation is the essence of their situation. Race, then, is an ideological misnomer that continues to hide the oppression of the African American nation just as it did in the heyday of evolutionary racist ideology.[2]

If, then, we replace the term *racist* with the terms "White nationalist" and "African American nationalist," a number of problems described previously can be avoided. First, "nationalism" will not be confused with prejudice. Second, as long as White nationalism (oppressing) is understood as the opposite of African American nationalism (liberating), the two cannot be equated. Third, the term racist can be reserved, as it should be, for those who are biological determinists. So, the term White nationalist includes all those White people who support the oppression of the African American nation whether knowingly or unknowingly. Color-blind liberals, color-blind conservatives, and old-style evolutionary racists are all White nationalists. Thus, all racists are White nationalists but not all White nationalists are racists. There is a fourth category of White people that is very rare. These are the people who reject both forms of African American oppression, color-blind and racist, and who support the right of African American people to self-determination.

A Modest Test

Some of the differences between Whites were examined in the author's study described previously (also in the Appendix). In this study, liberals were defined as those who said that they were color-blind and who supported affirmative action. They were 34 percent of the campus sample. Conservatives said they were color-blind but opposed affirmative action. They were 43 percent of the sample. Almost all of those who did not endorse color blindness were in the evolutionary racist category, defined as those who said they were not color-blind and also said that they opposed affirmative action. They were 16 percent of the sample. The remaining category had too few cases to analyze. This would have been the category of Whites who supported selfdetermination for African Americans. One would expect to find few such people on this campus in 1992.

Table A.1 in the Appendix shows that, among color-blind Whites, the conservatives, compared to liberals, were significantly more prejudiced and more inclined to endorse racist ideology (agree that Black people are genetically inferior in intelligence).

What, then, is the difference between conservatives and the old evolutionary racists? Racists, like the conservatives, reject affirmative action, but unlike conservatives, they also rejected color blindness. Table A.1 shows that racists are more prejudiced and endorse racist ideology more than conservatives.

What we see, then, is that the liberals are the least nationalist, the conservatives are intermediate, and the racists are the most nationalist.

As discussed earlier, color blindness is one form of White nationalist ideology. Justice Harlan made that clear and in this study the rejection of color blindness by the majority of African American students, described earlier, helps confirm it. The higher levels of prejudice and racist ideology of the conservatives, compared to the liberals, suggest a certain duplicity in the color blindness of the conservatives. This duplicity is not unlike that of the conservative intellectuals and Supreme Court justices who omitted that part of Justice Harlan's dissent that explained that a color-blind constitution was the way to preserve the dominance of the White nation.

Liberals, however, have never owned up to what affirmative action really is. It is not really about diversity and it is entirely too pluralistic to be consistent with the ideology of color blindness, as conservatives have correctly pointed out. It is about redistributing valuable opportunities. It takes from those who have and gives to those who do not. The problem is that it, along with integration in general, tends to treat things such as employment and admission to college as a zero sum game instead of including people by expanding valued opportunities for everybody. Such an expansion would have been socialist in nature, requiring tight government control over education, employment, and wages along with heavy taxes on the rich. What was done instead has exacerbated competition to the clear advantage of the capitalist class. This is why integration was the path taken to resolve the contradictions arising from the end of the Southern sharecropping system and why self-determination for African American people was never a consideration. This is why race relations are so bad, working people are still split by nationalist divisions, and the ruling class rules.

THE NEW ERA

The near-convergence of the "New Democrats" with the Republican party on issues such as affirmative action and welfare makes it clear we are now in a new era.

One important factor in all of this is the demise of communism. We recall that one of the reasons the American ruling class initiated the break-up of the old apartheid racial system was its crusade against communism. Today, the Soviet Union has collapsed and China has embraced the "capitalist road" to development. The United States no longer has to "clean up its act" at home to compete against communist influence in the world. If, for example, there are any objections in other countries to the huge increase in African Americans being put into prison, nobody in authority in this country seems to care. After all, with the demise of communism, President Bush proclaimed the arrival of "a new world order." At home and abroad, American capitalism has grown extraordinarily bold and aggressive.

Today, de jure segregation is gone and there is a significantly larger African American middle class. Class now divides the African American nation as never before. The NAACP has been reduced to scandal, debt, and irrelevance. The threat of revolution in America, such as it was, is long past. African American identification with Third World liberation struggles has vanished. Where there was once revolutionary Black nationalism there seems to be only "Black capitalism." Manning Marable (1995) has observed that:

One major factor in the demise of Black consciousness and identity was the materialism and greed inherent in the existing American political economy and secular society. By asking to be integrated into the existing structures of society, rather than demanding the basic transformation of the system, Blacks became hostage to their own ideological demands. "Inoculated with secular values emphasizing the individual instead of the community," Parker observes, "young Blacks rarely recognize each other as brother and sisters, or as comrades in the struggle. We're now competitors, relating to each other out of fear and mistrust." (P. 19)

The egalitarian movements of the 1960s and 1970s failed to solve the riddle of race; the slogan "Black and White Unite" was not realized. Today, the continuing division of African American and White working people still does what it did in colonial America. It enables the ruling class to maintain political hegemony and, now in new ways, tighten the screws on all working people.

Declining Income and Increasing Inequality

There has been a radical increase in economic inequality in the United States since the late 1960s. The rich have gotten much richer at the expense of working people, and White nationalism played a major role in bringing this about.

The economist, Lester Thurow (1995), has shown that between 1973 and 1993 the GDP (gross domestic product) grew by 20 percent. During this time the median income of working men declined by 11 percent while the income of the top 20 percent of male earners increased. Between 1980 and 1990, the after-tax income of the top 20 percent increased by 27 percent while that of the second 20 percent increased by 6 percent. The income of the third, fourth, and last 20 percent fell by 2 percent, 4 percent, and 9 percent, respectively (Macionis 1995:280).

The inequality of wealth (all valuable assets) increased along with the inequality of income. In 1973, the top 20 percent owned 76 percent of all wealth in the country (Robertson 1987). In 1990, they owned 80 percent (Macionis 1995:267). But within that group, the top 5 percent doubled their share of all wealth between the mid-1970s and the 1990s—from about 20 percent to over 40 percent (Thurow 1995). So, the rich got richer but the extremely rich got extremely richer. The bottom 40 percent of American families has little or no wealth, and the bottom 20 percent has negative wealth, or debt (Macionis 1995).

Nationalist Division, Competition, and Political Control

The essence of national oppression is found in the essence of capitalism, in the extraction of surplus value. The competitive nature of capitalism drives the capitalist to find the cheapest possible labor. The fundamental racist act occurs when the capitalist finds cheaper labor in some "alien" group and brings that group into competition with their existing employees. Unless there is a scarcity of labor, wages will fall when this is done. As previously discussed, if workers react against falling wages, they can direct their fear and anger in one of two directions—against the capitalist or, as racists, against the aliens. Workers tend to attack the aliens because they are weak, and the capitalist is protected by the state. For ideological reasons, those who try to explain racism almost always look at the reaction of workers rather than the primary act of the capitalist. Archie Bunker, the ignorant White working man, was vilified on television but there was no equivalent situation comedy about a capitalist. Now that Archie Bunker, the union man, is a Republican, liberals are in a quandary. But what should it be called when the capitalist acts to degrade or destroy the lives of his or her workers by seeking cheaper labor? "Prejudiced" hardly fits, capitalists are attracted to cheap labor all over the world. Slave owners, we recall, had a mighty attraction to African people. It is obviously an ideological phenomenon that we have no word to characterize this fundamental act of aggression that sets national oppression in motion. Instead, we talk about prejudice or racism.[3]

It is not a natural law that wages must fall when cheaper alien labor is put into competition with higher-paid workers. It is extremely probable that this will occur, but if the capitalist accumulates greater surplus value, he or she could use it to bring the wage rates of the new workers up to those of the old workers and also refrain from laying off the old workers. Then, there would be little or no racist (or sexist) worker reaction. But capitalism is not about philanthropy, it is about surplus value. Right now there is greatly increased competition and at the same time there is still the split-labor market in which African Americans (and women) are concentrated in certain poorly paid occupations sectors of the economy. Either way, national and gender oppression generates extra surplus value and capitalism gains. This is expressed politically in the way the capitalist class finances both parties, the Republicans (split labor) and the Democrats (integration) (see Lewis and the Center for Public Integrity 1996). White nationalist reaction has led to the election of a series of conservative presidents and to the phenomenon of the "New Democrats." This has led to policies that have made the condition of all working people, White and African American, worse, not better.

The Consequences of the Reagan Revolution

As we have shown, Richard Nixon and Ronald Reagan and George Bush each became president of the United States by making blatant and outrageous racist appeals to White workers. They attacked the government programs and employment that had been created to cope with the millions of African Americans who had not been incorporated into the privately owned economy. The message was that African Americans were living off the government and the taxpayers instead of going to work. By supporting this attack, White workers imagined that their race interests were being protected. This led to the "Reagan Revolution." Reagan and conservative Republicans and Democrats in Congress changed the tax code so that the rich paid no more than a 50 percent tax, and then in 1986, it was lowered to 28 percent, one of the lowest rates in the world (Robertson 1987:270). This gave 70 billion more to the rich while shifting the tax burden to the classes beneath them; it also drove up the budget deficit dramatically (Zinn 1995:568).

In addition, the Reagan Revolution contributed to the decline of labor unions. Unions are one of the primary means by which workers can improve their pay, benefits, working conditions, and influence government policies. Early in his administration, Reagan decided to deal with a strike of air traffic controllers by firing all those on strike (Zinn 1995:652), training new ones, hiring them, and refusing to take back any of those who had struck even after the strike had collapsed. He then proceeded to stack the National Labor Relations Board with pro-business officials who allowed the same tactics to be employed across the country. Eventually, the right to strike was virtually destroyed because strikers' jobs would be given to others. Between 1935 and 1950, unionized workers rose to one third of the labor force but declined to less than 16 percent of the labor force after the 1970s (Macionis 1995:418). The decline in union strength is a major factor in the increase of income inequality in the United States. White workers who voted out of White nationalist sentiment for Ronald Reagan should be able to understand that this cost them dearly, but apparently few if any see it this way.[4]

Immigrants

Steinberg (1989) has argued that in the past 25 years, 11 million legal immigrants have entered the United States while 3 million industrial jobs were created. Barlett and Steele (1996) say that immigration since 1990 has been at the highest level in this country's history, 6 million people. Blackwell (1991:88) noted that a survey in 1980 found that 80 percent of White and 82 percent of African American people wanted immigration curtailed. Immigration has been a source of resentment in the African American nation since the turn of the century (Du Bois 1935). Why, if "America" is committed to integrating African Americans into the labor force, has it brought about such a high level of immigration? Why are certain new immigrants included in the protected categories of affirmative action? Barlett and Steele report that Labor Department investigations indicate that regulations designed to protect American workers are easily and frequently circumvented by employers (Barlett and Steele 1996). Attacking immigrants, of course, instead of employers is a classic White nationalist diversion. Liberals, on the other hand, defend the immigrants without questioning the employers and the government policies that have exacerbated the competition for jobs between African Americans and other working people.

Women

Of course, women have also entered the labor force in unprecedented numbers. Continuing technological advancement has placed men and women on an equal footing for employment in many occupations. In 1960, 80 percent of men and 38 percent of women were in the labor force. In 1993, 75 percent of men and 58 percent of women were in the labor force. Nearly 60 percent of all married women are employed (Macionis 1995:368). Women of all races make up 40 percent of the labor force today and White women make up 40 percent of all middle-management positions (Marable 1995:86). In fact, White women have been the chief beneficiaries of affirmative action, especially in the better paying jobs (Hacker 1995:137; Sokoloff 1992). The wage gap between men and women has narrowed. This is because the wages of men have fallen toward the lower level of women, which has remained constant (Macionis 1995:280). People did not realize when they demanded "equal pay for equal work" that one way to achieve equal pay between men and women was to bring down the pay of men to the level of women.

The entry of married women into the labor market was the primary reason that median family income continued to rise, but that only lasted until 1989.[5] Family income has fallen 7 percent since that time (Thurow 1995). The affluence of the minority of upwardly mobile families is often explained by the presence of a professionally employed, well-educated female. What is often overlooked in the typical two-wage-earner household, however, is the additional expense in having a second earner—such as a second car, clothing, child care, travel, and so forth. Numerous newspaper and magazine articles have been written about the enormous strain that two-wage-earner parents experience trying to care for their children and the demands of their job schedules. To be sure, employment gave some women an alternative to patriarchal family life, but the big money winners in all of this are clearly the super rich.

Downsizing

Chief executive officers (CEOs) of major corporations are compensated with both salaries and stock (company ownership). In 1960, they received 12 times more than the lowest paid worker in their companies. In 1975, it was 35 times more and in 1995, it was 117 times more (Yates 1995b). Apparently the trend is continuing upward. A survey conducted of the 150 largest companies showed that CEO's income rose nearly 15 percent in 1996. With stock options, the increase in total compensation was up 31 percent to a median of 5 million dollars. This was double the rise in 1994 and triple the rise in 1993. It was noted that because CEO compensation is tightly tied to the value of stock, CEOs have frequently used "downsizing," or mass firings of workers, to boost stock values (Uchitelle 1996). For example, after AT&T announced the downsizing of 40,000 employees, its stock gained 4 billion dollars in market value (Will 1996). AT&T estimates that in the past decade 25,000 jobs have been transferred to Asia and Latin America (Barlett and Steele 1996).

Having defeated communism abroad, vast new areas of the world now lay open to capitalist exploitation where people will work for next to nothing. The export of American-made goods has doubled in the past 15 years, but imports have tripled. A significant part of imported goods are made by American manufactures who have moved production out of the country in the quest for low wages, and also retailers who manufacture little or nothing in the country (Barlett and Steele 1996).

Downsizing is a relatively new phenomenon that reflects the growing confidence of capital. Historically, "lay-offs" have been expected by blue-collar workers on the down side of the business cycle. Downsizing is being employed against all workers including large numbers of white-collar office workers and even managerial workers. It often occurs in corporations that are quite profitable.

Labor Department analysis showed that the higher the income, the lower the layoffs until the 1980s when the protection of higher income disappeared (Uchitelle and Kleinfield 1996).

The creation of new jobs has exceeded the loss of old jobs and the labor force has expanded by 32 percent since 1979 (Uchitelle and Kleinfield 1996). The problem is that many of the new jobs pay less than the old ones (Barlett and Steele 1996). Much of the growth has been in service and retail trades, which pay poorly and tend to employ temporary workers. The old industrial jobs primarily paid well because they were unionized. The new jobs pay poorly because they are not unionized. Many African American migrants arrived in the North just as good, unionized, industrial jobs were being shut down. These jobs employed 26 percent of labor force in 1960 but less than 15 percent today (Macionis 1995:282). The northeast and parts of the midwest became known as the "Rust Belt" as industries moved to the anti-union South or were moved abroad.

"Outsourcing" and "temporary workers" are two popular ways of reducing worker's pay and benefits and increasing corporate profits. Companies terminate jobs or even whole departments and contract the work outside the company with smaller enterprises. This may eliminate having to pay union wages, having to pay into pension and health funds, and so forth. Companies like Nike, Bugle Boy, and Mattel operate none of their own factories, for example (Pearlstein 1995). "Temps" provide the same kinds of reductions in labor costs. Manpower Inc., a temporary agency, is the largest employer in the United States today (Uchitelle and Kleinfield 1996). Temporary workers of all types now make up 30 percent of the total workforce (Macionis 1995:419).

Corporate mergers nearly always result in heavy job losses, and mergers have been taking place at a record rate. For example, the Chase Manhattan-Chemical Bank merger downsized one sixth of the workforce—12,000 out of 75,000 jobs were eliminated (Yates 1995a). In 1995, U.S. companies announced merger deals worth a record 466 billion dollars, which surpassed the 347 billion record set in 1994. In the past decade, one half of all businesses reduced their workforces. The estimate is that 3 million jobs have been lost to downsizing and mergers in the past 7 years (Ivins 1996).

Downsizing explains at least part of the decline of older men in the labor force. In 1949, 87.3 percent of men between the ages of 55 and 64 were working; it was 64.8 percent in 1994 (a drop of 22.5 percent). Employment of women in the same age group during the same time grew by 23.2 percent, no doubt working at lower wages (Flinn and Rogers 1995).

Fortune 500 companies have shed 25 percent of their employees in recent years but their sales, in inflation-adjusted dollars, have increased (Pearlstein 1995). In 1990, 43 percent of companies laying off workers gave "business downturn" as the sole cause. In 1995, it was 6 percent ("America Still Works" 1995).

Sixty-one percent of medium and big companies have ended the practice of giving annual merit raises to many of their employees. They now give "variable pay," which means that a worker's base pay is not raised but they may receive bonuses depending on the performance of the company. Apparently, companies have applied this policy to non-union workers and not the unionized ones (Lublin 1997).

The degradation of the white-collar worker has been bitterly satirized in the popular *Dilbert* comic strip. *Newsweek* ("Work Is Hell" 1996) featured the *Dilbert* phenomenon and suggested that work today was hell. Today, instead of offices, many people work in small cubicles, or "hotel" by sharing an office when they are in town. Similarly, some workers only work at home and have no office. Devices such as computers, fax machines, cellular phones, and beepers put millions of workers on call 24 hours a day. Overtime is at an all time high whereas vacation time has decreased because companies force surviving workers to do the jobs of those who were fired. Stress, fatigue, depression, and anxiety are said to be widespread (Hancock 1995).

In addition to the private sector, President Clinton claims to have eliminated 200,000 government jobs (Alter 1996). Clinton, like Presidents Bush and Reagan before him, has followed a conservative policy with regard to the growth of the economy. He has approved the policy of the Federal Reserve Board of increasing the interest rate at the slightest hint of inflation. By keeping economic growth at a comparatively low level, wages are suppressed because capitalists compete less with each other for workers (Baker 1995). Even though the unemployment rate has slowly fallen, the effects of slow economic growth combined with downsizing and the other factors described here, mean that people are working but they are working much harder for significantly less. There is no natural law that caused this to happen. Capitalists in America did this because they could get away with it. Finding no resistance, they push on.

For contrast, consider what happened in France in 1995 when the newly elected conservative government attempted to downsize the railway workers and made clear its intention to deal with other government workers in a similar fashion. The railway workers quickly went on strike, shutting down the rail system and paralyzing much of France. Unlike America, it is illegal to replace striking workers in France. Nineteen days later 2 million people took to the streets in support of the rail workers. After three weeks of accelerating demonstrations, the government withdrew its downsizing plans for the rail workers. But the communist-led General Confederation of Workers threatened more strikes unless working hours were reduced and the minimum wage raised above the current $1,000 a month. Marc Blondel, the head of Workers Force, proposed dealing with high unemployment in France by "sharing the work." National law mandates five weeks of vacation a year for all workers; Blondel proposed making it six weeks and reducing the current 39-hour work week to 35 hours ("France is Returning" 1995).

Europeans have enjoyed the benefits of a generous welfare state for many decades, through prosperity and recession. Despite economic difficulties in some European countries today, there appears little prospect that they will give it up (Nash 1996). A recent study showed that keeping wages high is not associated with high unemployment—some European countries have high unemployment while others do not. The United States is among the low-wage countries, and if its true rate of unemployment is calculated, not the rate based only on those actively seeking work, it is a country with a high rate of unemployment (Longworth 1996). The situation of working people in Europe is clearly superior to that of Americans. The reason is obvious—more than 50 percent of workers are in unions in Europe as a whole; in Scandinavian countries, 80 percent are unionized (Macionis 1995:418). These people simply do not accept the argument that solitary individuals must meet their fate in the "marketplace." They are organized to see that all get a reasonable share. Europeans have their racist politicians too, but they wield little influence.

In late 1996, and early 1997, government attempts at downsizing and reductions in social benefits have produced massive strikes and demonstrations in France, Belgium, England, and The Netherlands (Pomeroy 1996). Unions struck in Israel to protest budget cuts and privatization plans while a national strike occurred in Korea to thwart similar plans along with anti-union legislation ("20,000 South Koreans March in Protest" 1996). It appears that the American model for increasing the rate of surplus-value accumulation and inequality will not go so smoothly in all parts of the New World Order.

In short, in America, increased competition from legal and illegal immigrants, export of jobs to foreign workers, entry of African Americans and White women into new sectors of the job market, downsizing, outsourcing, increased use of temporary workers, replacement of older men, technological change such as computers, changes in tax laws, and the decline of unions all add up to one thing: The rich have gotten extraordinarily richer while the average working person has gotten not only poorer in income, but poorer in the quality of life.

White American workers, bereft of unions but full of White nationalism, now have their choice of agendas: the Republican color-blind and downsizing agenda or the "New Democratic" color-blind and downsizing agenda. Americans have the shortest annual vacation time in the industrial world— Brazilians get more (Stieghorst 1996). Americans have declining median incomes, greater work demands, extraordinary job insecurity, stress, fear, and anxiety. Their great compensation, however, will be the spectacle of millions of poor mothers with dependent children being thrown off of welfare, the end or the further crippling of affirmative action, attacks on immigrants, the ever-expanding incarceration of African American people, more frequent executions, and the assurance that Black English is not a language. Meanwhile, the rich rejoice all the way to the banks, which are being merged at an unprecedented rate.

NOTES

1. Heard by author at a speech in Akron, Ohio, in 1976.

2. African Americans are co-opted into the White nation to act against the interests of the African American nation as in the case of the appointment of Supreme Court Justice Clarence Thomas. Although many African Americans call him a "race traitor," it would be more accurate to call him a traitor to the African American nation. Thomas's race is African American, his nation is White. Conversely, Joe Slovo, a White, Communist member of the African National Congress in South Africa, was a traitor to the White oppressing nation. The "white nigger" in America, so named by White nationalists long ago, is a White person who is a traitor to the White nation. Today, according to my students, White students call their fellow White students who "hang out" with African Americans, or who adopt African American styles of dress and music, "whitegers."

3. The term "institutional racism" (Carmichael and Hamiliton 1967) was developed to try to differentiate racism in societal institutions from individual racism but it often meant nothing more than the prejudiced or racist acts of people running institutions such as banks, corporations, government agencies, and so forth. The view presented here makes national oppression systemic by locating racism in the base of capitalism, in the means of production.

4. President Clinton promised to pass legislation to reverse "labor replacement" but quickly gave up on the idea when he became president.

5. The economist, Robert Samuelson (1996), has criticized Barlett and Steele and similar journalistic inquiries. Samuelson says that adjustments for inflation are inaccurate and understate income. He argues that households today have more consumer goods than they did in 1980, and concludes that "people buy more because their incomes are higher." Here, Samuelson has erroneously equated household income with individual income. And, by going back to 1980, he combined a period when two-wage-earner family income was rising with the later period when it fell.

REFERENCES

Allen, Robert L. 1970. *Black Awakening in Capitalist America.* New York: Doubleday Anchor.
Alter, Jonathan. 1996. "Should We Rehire This Man?" *Newsweek,* September 2, pp. 37-43.
"America Still Works." 1995. *Harper's Magazine,* August.
Baker, Russell. 1995. "Poor Have to be among Us." *Virginian-Pilot,* January 20.
Barlett, Donald and James Steele. 1996. "Who Killed the American Dream"? *Virginian-Pilot,* September 22-28.
Benjamin, Lois. 1991. *The Black Elite: Facing the Color Line in the Twilight of the 20th Century.* Chicago: Nelson-Hall.
Blackwell, James. 1991. *The Black Community.* New York: HarperCollins.
Bryson, Chris. 1996. "Crime Pays for Those in the Prison Business." *National Times,* October, pp. 28-35.
Butler, Paul. 1995. "Racially Based Jury Nullification: Black Power in the Criminal Justice System." *Yale Law Journal,* December.
"California Senator Seeks Inquiry into Reported CIA-Backed Cocaine Sales." 1996. *Virginian-Pilot,* August 30.
Carmichael, Stokely and Charles V. Hamilton. 1967. *Black Power.* New York: Vintage.
Cose, Ellis. 1993. *The Rage of the Privileged Class.* New York: HarperCollins.
Diversity Project: Final Report. 1991. Berkeley, CA: Institute For the Study of Social Change.
Du Bois, W. E. B. 1935. *Black Reconstruction.* New York: Russell and Russell.
Edsall, Thomas B. and Mary D. Edsall. 1991. *Chain Reaction: The Impact of Race, Rights, and Taxes on American Politics.* New York: W. W. Norton.
Fanon, Franz. 1963. *The Wretched of the Earth.* New York: Grove.
Feagin, Joe R. and Melvin P. Sikes. 1994. *Living with Racism: The Black Middle-Class Experience.* Boston: Beacon.
Flinn, John and Dick Rogers. 1995. "Age: Older Men Disappearing from the Workforce." *Virginian-Pilot,* August 17, pp. D1-D2.
"France Is Returning to Normal, But Union Warns of New Strife." 1995. *Virginian-Pilot,* December 19, p. A4.
Frankenberg, Ruth. 1993. *White Women, Race Matters: The Social Construction of Whiteness.* Minneapolis: University of Minnesota Press.
Frazier, Franklin. 1963. *The Negro Church in America.* New York: Schocken.
Gadsden, V. and D. Wagner, eds. 1995. *Literacy among African American Youth: Issues in Learning, Teaching, and Schooling.* Cresskill, NJ: Hampton.

Guinier, Lani. 1994. *The Tyranny of the Majority.* New York: Free Press.
Hacker, Andrew. 1995. *Two Nations.* New York: Ballentine.
Hancock, LynNell. 1995. "Breaking Point." *Newsweek,* March 6, pp. 56-61.
hooks, bell. 1995. *Killing Rage.* New York: Henry Holt.
Ivins, Molley. 1996. "Survivors of Downsizing Suffer Too." *Virginian-Pilot,* February 12.
Jackson, Joe. 1995. "Judge Tosses Out Drug Indictments." *Virginian-Pilot,* December 22, pp. A1-A5.
Jones, Evonne Parker. 1991. "The Impact of Economic, Political, and Social Factors on Recent Overt Black-White Racial Conflict in Higher Education in the United States." *Journal of Negro Education* 60:524-37.
LaFay, Laura. 1996. "What's Going on in Virginia's Prisons?" *Virginian-Pilot,* September 3, pp. A1, A12.
Leland, John and Nadine Joseph. 1997. "Hooked on Ebonics." *Newsweek,* January 13, pp. 78-79.
Lewis, Anthony. 1996. "California Prisons: Hopefully, Not a Preview of All of America." *Virginian-Pilot,* March 27.
Lewis, Charles and Center For Public Integrity. 1996. *The Buying of the President.* New York: Avon.
Longworth, R. C. 1996. "Low Salaries in U.S. Not Keeping Down Jobless Rate, Study Says." *Virginian-Pilot,* August 25.
Lublin, Joann S. 1997. "Don't Count on Merit Raise in Your Paycheck in the Future." *Virginian-Pilot,* January 12, pp. D1-D2.
Macionis, John J. 1995. *Sociology.* New York: Prentice Hall.
Macionis, John J. 1997. *Sociology.* 6th ed. Upper Saddle River, NJ: Prentice Hall.
Marable, Manning. 1995. *Beyond Black and White: Transforming African American Politics.* New York: Verso.
Marger, Martin N. 1994. *Race and Ethnic Relations: American and Global Perspectives.* 3d ed. Belmont, CA: Wadsworth.
Massey, Douglas S. and Nancy A. Denton. 1993. *American Apartheid.* Cambridge, MA: Harvard University Press.
Nash, Nathaniel. 1996. "The Welfare State is Alive and Well in Western Europe." *New York Times News Service,* January 2, p. C8.
"Oakland to Change Wording of Ebonics Plan." 1997. *Virginian-Pilot,* January 13, p. A2.
Ola, Akinshiju. 1981. "Black Meet Discusses Strategy." *Guardian,* December 16, p. 7.
Pearlstein, Steven. 1995. "Restructuring Creates the 'Virtual Corporation.' " *Virginian-Pilot,* December 14, pp. D1, D6.
"Philadelphia Police Scandal Jolts Justice System, Negates Reform." 1995. *Los Angeles Times,* October 21, p. A26.
Pomeroy, William. 1996. "French Strike Highlights Fight Against Capitalist Plan for Europe." *People's Weekly World,* January 6.
"Prisons Nationwide See Record One-Year Increase, Study Says." 1995. *Virginian-Pilot,* April 4, p. A2.
"Racial Overtones Color GOP Reforms, Some Say." 1995. *Virginian-Pilot,* February 19, p. A6.
Robertson, Ian. 1987. *Sociology.* 3d ed. New York: Worth.
Rosenthal, A. M. 1996. "Resolve to Treat Criminals or Risk Losing Drop in Crime Benefits." *Virginian-Pilot,* January 12.
Rowan, Carl. 1996. *The Coming Race War in America.* New York: Little, Brown.
Samuelson, Robert. 1996. "Confederacy of Dunces." *Newsweek,* September 23, p. 65.

"75 Percent of Maryland Drug Patrol's Stops Are of Blacks." 1996. *Virginian-Pilot,* May 23, p. A2.

"Sheriff Puts First Female Chain Gang to Work." 1996. *Virginian-Pilot,* September 20, p. A8.

Simpson, George Easton and J. Milton Yinger. 1972. *Racial and Cultural Minorities: An Analysis of Prejudice and Discrimination.* 4th ed. New York: Harper and Row.

Sokoloff, Natalie. 1992. *Black Women and White Women in the Professions.* New York: Routledge, Chapman, and Hall.

Steinberg, Stephen. 1989. *The Ethnic Myth.* Boston: Beacon.

Stieghorst, Tom. 1996. "U.S. Vacation Time Falls Short." *Virginian-Pilot,* July 15.

"Study: 1 in 3 Young Black Men Are Serving a Criminal Sentence." 1995. *Virginian-Pilot,* October 5, p. A4.

Thurow, Lester. 1995. "Workers' Wages Continue to Fall." *Virginian-Pilot,* November 19.

"Tougher Laws Send Prisons Scrambling for Added Space." 1996. *Virginian-Pilot,* August 19, p. A1.

"20,000 South Koreans March in Protest." 1996. *Virginian-Pilot,* December 30.

Uchitelle, Louis. 1996. "Executive Pay Up Nearly 15 Percent at Many Big Firms." *Virginian-Pilot,* March 30.

Uchitelle, Louis and N. R. Kleinfield. 1996. "Americans are Being Forced to Downsize Their Expectations." *Virginian-Pilot,* March 10.

"Warden Fired for Plan on Female Chain Gang." 1996. *Virginian-Pilot,* April 27.

"Wave of Church Burnings a Sign of Rising Racism, Officials Say." 1996. *Virginian-Pilot,* November 10.

Wellman, David T. 1993. *Portraits of White Racism.* Cambridge, MA: Cambridge University Press.

Whitaker, Mark. 1995. "Whites v. Blacks." *Newsweek,* October 16, pp. 28-35.

Will, George. 1996. "Arguing About the Economy." *Virginian-Pilot,* March 5.

Wilson, William Julius. 1994. *The Political Economy and Urban Racial Tensions.* Memphis, TN: P. K. Seidman Foundation.

"Work is Hell." 1996. *Newsweek,* August 12.

Yates, Ronald. 1995a. "Most See Merger Mania as the Way to Adapt to the New World Order." *Virginian-Pilot,* September 7.

Yates, Ronald. 1995b. "CEO." *Virginian-Pilot,* October 12, pp. D1, D2.

Zinn, Howard. 1995. *A People's History of the United States: 1492-Present.* New York: Harper Perennial.

APPENDIX:
SYMBOLIC RACISM LITERATURE

In the 1970s, a series of studies of public attitudes showed that traditional expressions of anti-African American prejudice were becoming much less common in the United States (Campbell 1971; Greeley and Sheatsley 1971; Taylor, Sheatsley, and Greeley 1978). But studies also showed that opposition was very high among Whites to policies such as affirmative action (Lipset and Schneider 1978) and busing children to achieve school desegregation (Kelly 1974). These were policies that could actually address the problems of racial inequality and provide some degree of amelioration. The widespread opposition to these policies led some to argue that a new kind of racism was developing, "symbolic" or "modern" racism (McConahay and Hough 1976; McConahay, Hardee, and Batts 1981; Kinder and Sears 1985; Sears, Hensler, and Speer 1979; Sears and Kinder 1971). The symbolic racist was said to have a negative affect toward African American people that was not expressed in traditional ways, but as an irrational opposition to things such as affirmative action and busing (McConahay and Hough 1976). Weigel and Howes (1985) found, however, that symbolic racism was highly correlated with an updated, multidimensional measure of anti-African American prejudice. In 1983, Bobo questioned the research that had found self-interest to be of little importance in determining racially oriented behavior such as opposition to busing. He also noted that some research on symbolic racism had operationalized the concept with political or ideological questions concerning t̶h̶ ̶ ̶ ̶ ̶ ̶u̶c̶h̶ ̶a̶s̶ affirmative action, welfare dependency, and so forth (Bobo 1983:1201). In 1986, Sniderman and Tetlock attacked the logic of much of the research on symbolic racism arguing that it was tautological, that cause was confused with effect. One cannot simply assert that opposition to affirmative action, for example, is racist, they said—that must be demonstrated. They argued that it is prejudice, an old phenomenon, that is the key to understanding the opposition of racists to affirmative action. They cited a number of surveys indicating that prejudice was still very strong even if it had diminished. On the other hand, they argued, there are people who oppose affirmative action who are not racists at all. These nonracists who oppose affirmative action may do so because they are "color-blind." They state the following:

> Perhaps the respondent objects out of belief that color-blind decision-making procedures provide the fairest method of guaranteeing equality of opportunity (or social harmony) in the long run. (Sniderman and Tetlock 1986:146)

Sniderman later distanced himself from this position and attacked "individualism" as an "ungenerous" idea (Sniderman and Hagen 1985).

Several of the researchers trying to identify a new racism have argued that new racists have found a self-serving justification for their opposition to things such as affirmative action by reference to such things as the violation of "cherished American values" (McConahay and Hough 1976:23), and to "individualism and self-reliance, the work ethic, obedience, and discipline" (Kinder and Sears 1985:416).

Roth (1990:29), however, has taken great exception to this argument. As Sniderman and Tetlock (1986) did earlier, Roth pointed out that the Kinder and Sears (1985) measure of symbolic racism scores respondents as racist because they oppose affirmative action and busing. How do they know that those who oppose these things are racists and not "simply upholders of traditional values," asked Roth. The only independent validation was a correlation with being conservative and voting Republican, which was no validation at all from his perspective (p. 31). Roth claimed that, " 'Symbolic racism,' then, is a phantom conjured up to substitute for a racism that has declined in significance" (p. 32). He goes on to say that:

> People may oppose busing and quotas because they believe them to endanger society by fostering group resentment and promoting inter group hostility. . . . (People) might honestly consider quotas and busing unwise and counterproductive. (P. 34)

Jackman and Muha (1984) found that education had little effect on negative attitudes toward African American people. Education was not significantly related to support for affirmative action. The authors departed from the data and speculated on the role that ideology might have in explaining these attitudes. They state the following:

> Yet individualism provides a general, principled, seemingly neutral basis for the rejection of aggregate group demands. The rights of the individuals are endorsed vehemently, as there is a systematic aversion to any representation of social problems in group terms. (P. 760)

Jackman and Muha (1984) saw this as ideology, which they said "flows naturally from their (White) side of experience" (p. 759). They speculated that the well educated prefer to base their opposition to affirmative racial policies on things such as individualism rather than on categorical racial distinctions. Their education makes them more "sophisticated." Unfortunately, there was no measurement of individualism or any other ideology in this study. In a related study, McClelland and Auster (1990) examined prejudice and social distance on a college campus. They found no prejudice at all among White students with the first measure and very little with the second but they did find large differences in the social distance. Using Jackman and Muha's example, they interpreted social distance as "reflecting" ideology although they, too, did not measure ideology. They repeated the argument that the role of prejudice has been replaced by ideology.

In brief, the research on a new racism started out with the notion that irrationalism was being expressed "symbolically" in opposition to policies such as affirmative action. Serious logical and measurement problems existed in this research. Conservative critics capitalized on these errors and defended opposition to affirmative action and busing as "honest" and not racist. Later research on a new racism made reference to more rational, political, or ideological explanations. But the argument that ideology explains opposition to affirmative action has remained essentially an argument because ideology was not measured in these studies.

SURVEY

In the fall of 1992, I conducted a survey of African American and White students attending a midsized university located in a mid-Atlantic southern state. A statistical profile of the student body was used to design a quota sample of full-time undergraduates according to academic division, class year, and sex. Approximately one out of 20 White students and one out of 5 African American students were interviewed. A sample of this type is appropriate for testing hypotheses, which is the purpose of this study (Sudman 1966). Members of a sociology honors class sought out students according to the criteria mentioned here and gave them sealed questionnaires. If those students declined, others with the same characteristics were substituted. Of 700 questionnaires collected, 619 were complete enough to use. The questions were presented to respondents in conventional five-choice Likert-type form. The items that follow were scored from the White perspective. All the variables except color blindness were scored so that the White nationalist response (in parentheses) had the higher score. For the color-blind variable, the liberal response (agree) was given the higher score to maintain conceptual and logical consistency.

* * *

Survey of Campus Attitudes

Color-Blind Ideology (cb)
1. I'm color-blind when it comes to race. (agree)

End Affirmative Action (end_affir)
1. Affirmative action should be ended. (agree)

Evolutionary Racist Ideology (race_iq)
1. I think that the average Black person is genetically inferior in intelligence to the average White person. (agree)

Prejudice Scale (prejud)
1. There are some White people that really make me uncomfortable because of what they say about Black people. (disagree)
2. People who can't laugh at a racist joke in private are just too liberal for me. (agree)
3. I personally prefer to socialize with members of my own racial group. (agree)

* * *

TABLE A.1 Correlation Matrix, White Respondents

	lib_con	con_evo	prejud	race_iq
lib_con	–			
con_evo	–	–		
prejud	0.2514	0.4663	–	
	0.0004	0.0000		
	198	153		
race_iq	0.2021	0.3391	0.4638	–
	0.0043	0.0000	0.0000	
	198	153	451	

NOTE: lib_con (liberal = 0, conservative = 1), con_evo (conservative = 0, racist = 1), prejud (prejudice scale, higher score = greater prejudice), race_iq (strongly disagree = 1, disagree = 2, don't know = 3, agree = 4, strongly agree = 5).

Agreeing that one is color-blind means that the respondent subscribes to that ideology. The question on "Black" intelligence operationalized the evolutionary racist ideology as developed by 19th-century ideologists. The items for the prejudice scale were selected from a larger set of questions that were subjected to factor analysis. Only one underlying factor was present. The prejudice scale had an alpha of .59 with an average interitem covariance of .41. This is adequate for the purposes of testing hypotheses. The actual scales used were created by a set of new variables that are estimates of the first k factors produced by rotation (see Stata 1993:332). In the follow-up study described next, this prejudice scale again had an alpha of .59. It correlated .62 (.0001) with a second measure of prejudice described here.

Liberals were defined as those who said they were color-blind and who also said they supported affirmative action. Conservatives were defined as those who said they were color-blind but said they opposed affirmative action. The difference between liberals and conservatives in terms of prejudice and racist ideology was tested by constructing a dummy variable in which *liberal* was equal to 0 and *conservative* was equal to 1. Racists were defined as those who said that they were not color-blind and who were also opposed to affirmative action. The difference between conservatives and racists was tested with the a dummy variable in which *conservative* was equal to 0 and *racist* was equal to 1. The results are shown in Table A.1.

FOLLOW-UP STUDY

A follow-up study was conducted on the same campus in the spring of 1996. Questionnaires were passed out in an introductory sociology class and an introductory biology class. There were 151 usable questionnaires returned completed by Whites and 52 questionnaires completed by African Americans. After being asked some of the questions contained in the first study, students were asked to write out their answers to the following questions:

1. Some people say they are "color-blind" when it comes to race and other people say they are not "color-blind." People may mean different things when they talk about "color blindness" and race. Can you explain what the term "color blindness" means to you?

2. Can you explain why you are either color-blind or not color-blind when it come to race? Or why you don't know?

Responses to the questions are described in Chapter 8.

In addition to these questions, students were asked to respond to the three-item prejudice scale used in the first study and also to a five-item scale used in a study by McClendon (1985). McClendon (1985) selected these five items from several scales used to measure prejudice in earlier studies. In the follow-up study, the five items had an alpha of .77. The items included the following:

1. How would you feel if a member of your family wanted to bring a Black friend home to dinner?

2. Do you think there should be a law against marriages between Blacks and Whites?

3. White people have a right to keep Blacks out of their neighborhoods and Blacks should respect that right.

4. Some people feel that Blacks should not push themselves where they are not wanted.

5. How would you feel if a Black family moved into your block?

REFERENCES

Bobo, Lawrence. 1983. "White's Opposition to Busing: Symbolic Racism or Realistic Group Conflict?" *Journal of Personality and Social Psychology* 45:1196-210.

Campbell, A. 1971. *White Attitudes Toward Black People.* Ann Arbor, MI: Institute for Social Research.

Greeley, A. M. and P. B. Sheatsley. 1971. "Attitudes Toward Racial Integration." *Scientific American* 222:13-19.

Jackman, Mary R. and Michael J. Muha. 1984. "Education and Intergroup Attitudes: Moral Enlightenment, Superficial Democratic Commitment, or Ideological Refinement?" *American Sociological Review* 49:751-69.

Kelly, J. 1974. "The Politics of School Busing." *Public Opinion Quarterly* 38:23-39.

Kinder, D. R. and D. O. Sears. 1985. "Prejudice and Politics: Symbolic Racism Versus Racial Threats to the Good Life." *Public Interest* 98:26-36.

Lipset, S. M. and W. Schneider. 1978. "The Bakke Case: How Would It Be Decided at the Bar of Public Opinion." *Public Opinion* 1:38-44.

McClelland, K. E. and Carol J. Auster. 1990. "Public Platitudes and Hidden Tensions." *Journal of Higher Education* 61:607-42.

McClendon, McKee. 1985. "Racism, Rational Choice, and White Opposition to Racial Change: A Case Study of Busing." *Public Opinion Quarterly* 49:214-33.

McConahay, J. B. and J. C. Hough. 1976. "Symbolic Racism." *Journal of Social Issues* 32:23-45.

McConahay, J. B., B. B. Hardee, and V. Batts. 1981. "Has Racism Declined in America?" *Journal of Conflict Resolution* 25:563-80.

Roth, Byron. 1990. "Social Psychology's 'Racism.' " *Public Interest* 98(1): 26-36.

Sears, D. O., C. P. Hensler, and L. K. Spear. 1979. " 'Whites' Opposition to 'Busing.' " *American Political Science Review* 73:369-84.

Sears, D. O., and D. R. Kinder. 1971. "Racial Tensions and Voting in Los Angeles." In *Los Angeles: Viability and Prospects for Metropolitan Leadership,* edited by W. Z. Hirsch. New York: Praeger.

Sniderman, Paul M. and M. Hagen. 1985. *Race and Inequality.* New York: Chatham House.

Sniderman, Paul M. and Philip E. Tetlock. 1986. "Symbolic Racism: Problems of Motive Attribution in Political Analysis." *Journal of Social Issues* 42(2): 129-50.

Stata Corporation. 1993. *Stata Reference Manual: Release 3.1.* 6th ed. College Station, TX: Author.

Sudman, S. 1966. "Probability Sampling with Quotas." *Journal of the American Statistical Association* 61:749-71.

Taylor, D. G., P. B. Sheatsley, and A. M. Greeley. 1978. "Attitudes Toward Racial Integration." *Scientific American* 238(6): 42-9.

Weigel, Russell H. and Paul W. Howes. 1985. "Conceptions of Racial Prejudice: Symbolic Racism Reconsidered." *Journal of Social Issues* 41(3): 117-38.

INDEX

EDITOR'S NOTE: Page references followed by *t* or *f* indicate tables or figures, respectively.
Page references followed by "n" indicate endnotes.

ABOUT THE AUTHOR

Leslie G. Carr, Ph.D., University of North Carolina at Chapel Hill, is currently Associate Professor at Old Dominion University. He is the former Director of the Institute for the Study of Minority Issues at that university. His research interests and publications are primarily in the areas of African American/White relations, school segregation, low-income housing, and social theory.